NAYANTARA SAHGAL
AND
DORIS LESSING

NAYANTARA SAHGAL AND DORIS LESSING

A FEMINIST STUDY IN COMPARISON

NEENA ARORA

PRESTIGE

Published by
Prestige Books
3/28, East Patel Nagar, New Delhi 110 008
in association with
Indian Society for Commonwealth Studies
New Delhi

ISBN: 81-85218-31-5

Phototypesetting by
Laser Impressions
New Delhi 110 028
Ph. 537296, 537756

Jacket design by
Three-A Corporation
New Delhi 110 002

Printed at
Mehra Offset Press
New Delhi 110 002

Contents

To the memory

of

my mother

Preface

Women constitute about half the world's total population but their share in various areas of activity has been totally disproportionate to their numerical strength. For centuries, they have been denied full justice – social, economic, political and constitutional and largely ignored as the "weaker sex." The mid-twentieth century saw the upsurge of a new awareness about the women's marginalised position resulting into the birth of Women's Liberation Movement. Literature, being the mirror of society, does not remain unaffected but explores the "woman's question" extensively and vociferously. In recent times, the question of the relative status of men and women has often engaged the attention of the authors all over the world.

Nayantara Sahgal, an outstanding Indian English writer, and her western counterpart Doris Lessing articulate their deep concern over gender-oppression in their works. Though Sahgal and Lessing belong to different countries, different societies and different cultures, yet one finds in their works continuity and similarity by which both imagine and convey the battle of the sexes.

This book seeks to interpret some selected works of Sahgal and Lessing from the Feminist perspective. Whatever the reception of the book, I hope it will be understood in the spirit in which it is offered as an attempt to interpret a subject of great importance in the context of contemporary social reality.

Shimla

Neena Arora

Introduction

Nayantara Sahgal is undoubtedly an outstanding Indian English novelist and an established political columnist. Born in Allahabad on May 10, 1927, she is the second of three daughters of Ranjit Sitaram Pandit and Vijaya Lakshmi Pandit. Nayantara spent her childhood in Anand Bhawan at Allahabad with her parents, her maternal uncle, Pt. Jawahar Lal Nehru, and her cousin Mrs. Indira Gandhi. Her father Ranjit Sitaram Pandit was a lawyer by profession, but left practice to join the Indian National Movement and later died of a serious illness soon after his release from jail in 1944. After her schooling at Mussorie, she alongwith her sister went to America and did her B.A. in History from Wellesley College, Massachusetts, in 1947. She married Gautam Sahgal in 1949, a young man working in a British Company, and had three children. It was a love marriage but it failed and she divorced Gautam in 1967. In 1979 she married again an I.C.S. officer, Mangat Rai, after many years of living together. Talking about her second marriage, she says: "Neither of us were at all interested in getting married. But in 1979, the Janata government appointed me ambassador to Italy and that forced me to marry. . . . Fundamentally, there is not much difference between living together and being married. If you are loyal to each other, it does not matter. If there is a loyalty and trust, one does not need marriage."[1] Nayantara saw politics from inside and was immensely influenced by the loving, sacrificing, refined and bold personalities of her father, mother and Pt. Jawahar Lal Nehru. She gives a memorable account of childhood impressions on her tender mind in her two autobiographies. Her first literary work was in fact her autobiography, *Prison and Chocolate Cake*, published in 1954. Subsequently her first novel, *A Time to be Happy*, appeared in 1957. Since then she has consistently been engaged in writing novels and political columns in newspapers.

Sahgal's literary canon consists of eight novels, two autobiographies, some non-fictional works, and several articles and short stories published in leading newspaper magazines. Her recent novels *Rich Like Us* (1985) and *Plans for Departure* (1986) have reinforced her position as one of the foremost Indian novelists on the contemporary scene. Her talent can be seen in full bloom in her *Rich Like Us* for wl ich she has received the prestigious British honour, the Sinclair Prize for Fiction; subsequently she was honoured with a Sahitya Akademi Award for the same novel. For her *Plans for*

Departure too, she has been awarded the Commonwealth Writer's Prize for Eurasia region. Her latest publication is a novel, *The Mistaken Identity* (1988), which too has been widely acclaimed by the critics.

Doris Lessing, the celebrated English Writer, was born of British parents in Kermanshah, Persia, on October 22, 1919. Her father Alfred Cook Taylor worked for the Imperial Bank of Persia in Tehran. The family emigrated to Southern Rhodesia, to the town of Banket, when she was five, and here she spent her childhood on a large farm. She got her first job, which was in a lawyer's office, at the age of sixteen. In 1939 she married Frank Wisdom. The marriage lasted for four years and two children, John and Jean, were the offspring of it. The second man she married was Gottfried Lessing – a half Jewish German immigrant to Rhodesia. Out of this wedlock, Peter, a son, was born in 1947. Her second marriage also ended in a fiasco. Doris Lessing left Rhodesia in 1949 for England where she and her son settled while Gottfried went to East Germany. In 1950, her first novel *The Grass is Singing* was published which became an immediate success. Her literary outpourings are quite amazing: she has written more than eighteen novels, ten collections of short-stories, a number of plays, poems and some non-fictional works and an autobiography *Going Home*.

While Nayantara Sahgal belongs to one of the aristocratic and elite families of India, Doris Lessing is the daughter of a banker, who first left London and came to Persia and then went to Rhodesia for his livelihood and struggled hard in life as a farmer. In Rhodesia, Doris along with her parents lived in real poverty in a pole and mud house which was family home for twenty years. Lessing has described this house in her book, *Going Home*, as like a "living thing, responsive to every mood of the weather; and during the time I was growing up it had already begun to sink back into the forms of the bush. I remember it as a rather old, shaggy animal standing still among the trees, lifting its head to look out over the lives and valleys to the mountains."[2] When Doris was sixteen, she left her studies and came out in the world of struggle and challenges and started her career as a typist in an office.

Despite their contrasting family backgrounds and different socio-cultural milieus, Sahgal and Lessing have had certain similar experiences as women in their respective married lives. Both the women have had unhappy marriages ending in divorces. About her marriage, Lessing recalls: "I married in my teens, when I was far too young, and had two children. That marriage was a failure and I married again. Let's put it this way: I do not think that marriage is one of my talents. I've been much happier unmarried than married."[3] While Doris Lessing went for divorce twice, Nayantara Sahgal had her divorce after seventeen years of her married life. Talking about her unfortunate matrimonial alliance, Sahgal regrets: "I should not really have married when I did. I don't think I was cut out to marry young. One should take time to decide. I should and would have left marriage for much later. But society in India pressurizes girls to marry young."[4] The personal agonies and traumas are reflected in the works of both the women writers, and the dissolution of marriage becomes one of the major themes in their works.

Both Lessing and Sahgal are still actively engaged in the creative process. Both started their literary career in the same decade; Lessing's first novel *The Grass is Singing* was written in 1950 and Sahgal's first literary work, her autobiography, *Prison and Chocolate Cake*, was published in 1954. Writing is a passion for them and both of them are writers with a vision of future. Discussing the role of an artist, Sahgal writes that a writer "has a mission... he has to create a vision of the future, he has to have a dream of his own and to suggest possibilities from it, I think it's the artist's job and the writer's job particularly in any society to show the way."[5]

Nayantara Sahgal was born and brought up in a family of patriots and self-sacrificing freedom fighters. Her parents, her maternal uncle, her maternal grandfather were all men of letters and wealthy debonairs. But they shed all pomp and show and devoted themselves (with Mahatama Gandhi) to the struggle for freedom of India. She has seen the turmoil both before and after the independence in 1947. Sahgal writes in her autobiography *Prison and Chocolate Cake*: "Our growing up was India's growing up into political maturity – a different kind of political maturity from any that the world has seen before, based on an ideology inspired by self-sacrifice, compassion and peace."[6] In her novels, on the one hand she exposes the power-hungry politicians and their madness for power, and on the other hand, she highlights the sincere freedom fighters's sacrifices for their motherland. She says: "the heroes in my novels were patterned on pre-independence examples and the villains on contemporary personalities."[7] In all her works there is a juxtaposition of two worlds: the personal world of man-woman relationship and the impersonal world of politics. Her works are marked with a humanistic vision and in her writings, as Jasbir Jain also observes, there is a "genuine concern for human values and human beings."[8] Her observations of the universal behaviour and reactions of the people, her mild humour and her depiction of the changing social conditions in contemporary India are quite interesting.

Doris Lessing has closely seen the times of the Second World War. Hence, the outcome of the brutal war, the violence and destruction, the decline of the civilization, the fragmentation of society are some of the recurrent themes in her novels. She examines the apartheid and the slow awakening among the black natives in the African colonies from the grass-roots level. Her hatred of the "white supremacy" is well brought out in her works. Lessing's fiction is remarkable for its encyclopaedic range and complexity. Lessing has equally well handled complex subjects like the "writer's block" and "schizophrenia," and in her recent novels she deals with "inner space," etc. In some of her works she talks of Sufism – the strengthening of a belief in the mind (above and beyond material conditions). She trenchantly depicts the alienation of man in a world imperilled by violence, and in her characters there is always a quest for some kind of wholeness and connectedness in life. Michael Thorpe perhaps rightly observes that Lessing is "the most accomplished, versatile and illuminating white African writer in English we have seen, or are likely to see."[9]

Like Nayantara Sahgal who could never forget her own country, her childhood imbued with the spirit of nationalism, even when she was out of her country, studying in U.S.A., Lessing never forgets Rhodesia and its landscapes where she spent her childhood and from where she came out finally to settle down in London. The country where she spent the earlier part of her life finds a significant place in her novels. Her evocation of the atmosphere and landscapes in Africa, the vegetation, animal life, forests with all the smells and hues, is brilliant and vivid. The African Veld has a deep symbolic significance in Lessing's works.[10] Sahgal captures the sight and sound of the rivers, the flora and fauna of the mountains, the nature in all its splendour, and makes it real and tangible in her fiction.

Sahgal and Lessing both have been accused of relating their "personal problems" in their works and the word "autobiographical" is often applied to their works by way of adverse criticism. Among others, Florence Howe says: "Doris Lessing's life is the source of her fiction."[11] Lessing, however, counters it: "I get impatient with this thing about "Autobiographical." You can't write about anything you haven't experienced, or imagined – it has to be your experience, your imagination . . . writers pick up ideas that are in the air – like an invisible wavelength of ideas."[12] In her Preface to *The Golden Notebook*, she puts her case more formally: "Writing about oneself, one is writing about others, since your problems, pains, pleasures, emotions – and your extraordinary and remarkable ideas – can't be your alone. The way to deal with the problem of 'subjectivity' . . . is to see him [i.e. the individual] as a microcosm and in this way to break through the personal, the subjective, making the personal general, as indeed life always does, transforming a private experience . . . into something much larger: growing up is after all only the understanding that one's unique and incredible experience is what everyone shares."[13]

The apparent slice of autobiography is traced in Sahgal's works too. And there are shadows of real life characters and incidents in her novels. For example, *The Day in Shadow* deals, as she herself says in an interview, with her "own life's experience."[14] Nevertheless, to view her works totally as subjective is erroneous, since like Lessing she too has sucessfully transformed personal experience into general ones. Sahgal is of the opinion that "everything around the writer is material for a novel. . . . All one's material comes from real life . . . one generally draws on one's own experience or someone else's experience."[15]

Further, Lessing and Sahgal both excel in delineating political, psychological and personal turmoils and study them with keen perception and deep insight. Above all, it is their almost uncanny grasp of human relations, their concern about the gender oppression and their subtle exposure of the marginalized and repressed position of woman in a male-dominated society, which bring them closer to each other.

The proposed dissertation aims at making a comparative study of Nayantara Sahgal's and Doris Lessing's selected works from the Feminist perspective. While Sahgal's five novels, viz., *This Time of Morning*, *Storm in Chandigarh*, *The Day in Shadow*, *A Situation in New Delhi* and *Rich Like Us* have been taken up, Lessing's five earlier novels, *The Grass is Singing*, *The Golden Notebook*, *Martha Quest*, *A Proper Marriage* and *A Ripple from the Storm* have been selected, because these resemble Sahgal's works more closely in terms of themes, characters, situations, etc. The comparative study of the two women novelists will reveal certain similarities in their handling of "woman's question" in a sexist society and thus will add to our understanding of the two authors. In analyzing the similarities in the two authors from the countries so different as England and India, the dissertation aims at bringing out the basic underlying experience common to all women transcending the barriers of class, colour or creed, thus suggesting the possibilities of international and cultural amity and understanding.

Various studies of Doris Lessing and Nayantara Sahgal separately have been made from different perspectives. Each of them has also been studied in comparison with other authors. For example, Doris Lessing has been compared with D. H. Lawrence, Margaret Atwood, Nadine Gordimer and Mary McCarthy, and Nayantara Sahgal has been compared with Anita Desai, Kamala Markandaya and Arun Joshi. Yet so far there has not been any comparative study of Doris Lessing and Nayantara Sahgal focusing on their handling of feminist issues in their works.

The position of women in any given society can be taken as a mark of the progress of civilization or, to use the words of Juliet Mitchell, as the "index of human advance."[16] Equality between the sexes as a principle – never as a practice – has been an essential part of the social or political ideologies at least in all democratic societies. Feminists are concerned with all kinds of oppression against women which they trace in patriarchy, and they insist on acceptance of women as equal beings. Feminism, as Charlotte Bunch says, is not simply "a laundry list of so-called women's issues such as child care and equal pay. While these issues are important, feminism is not a new ghetto where women are confined, to be concerned about only a select list of topics separated from the overall social and economic context of our lives. Similarly, feminism is not just an 'add women and stir' into existing institutions, ideologies, or political parties as they are."[17] It is a transformational politics which virtually touches on every aspect of our life. While some feminists stress the social and economic disadvantages of women and seek to change and improve women's immediate circumstances, and demand, for instance, equal pay, equal education, and job opportunities and also financial and legal independence for women, others seek to abolish the moral and spiritual superiority of one sex over the other. These feminists fight to end the subjection of women and to eradicate the existing gender discrimination.

Sahgal's women (like Sahgal herself) largely hail from the affluent class and do not experience much discrimination in educational or political fields and also do not aspire for financial independence. Lessing's protagonists mainly spring from the white privileged class, and are thus free from racial discrimination or oppression. As such she also does not focus much on economic and political freedom for women but rather takes them for granted. Both are, however, deeply and sensitively alive to women's predicament in a patriarchal society. In Sahgal and in Lessing, the struggle is for abolishing gender discrimination and seeking reciprocity, mutuality and harmony in life. When they assert women's strength and values, they do not propogate a separate "female world." but envision an organized whole world blending female virtues, morality and values with male culture so as to save it from catastrophe and doom.

In order to study the personal power relationships between the sexes in the works of Sahgal and Lessing, this dissertation is divided into four main chapters: (1) Feminism, (2) Woman Made Woman, (3) Woman as Wife, and (4) Free Woman?

The first chapter makes a historical survey of the subordinate position of women and their exploitation in various ways. It also studies the genesis and different stages and strands of Women's Liberation Movement and how it has affected the ethos, literature and criticism in our time.

The subsequent three chapters analyze the novels to study woman's position in different phases of her life. "Woman Made Woman" deals with an analysis of Sahgal's and Lessing's works in the light of the feminists's conviction that femininity is constructed culturally, not biologically. An attempt has been made to see how woman is groomed for a subordinate role and how her personality is conditioned into a secondary role right from childhood.

"Woman as Wife" has been divided into several sub-sections to study different aspects of a woman's oppression and suffering in marriage:

(i) Status of woman in marriage.
(ii) Double standards.
(iii) Violence and loneliness.
(iv) Attitude to love and marriage.
(v) Woman and motherhood.
(vi) Awareness towards emancipation.

The last chapter focuses on another phase of woman's struggle i.e. after divorce. The repercussions of divorce are discussed at length. Ironically, the emancipated woman fails to fulfil her commitment to herself and her arduous struggle for happiness still continues.

The final analysis of the various issues of feminism in the work of Sahgal and Lessing is given in the "Conclusion."

NOTES

1. Vijay Dutt and Harinder Baweja, "Nayantara Sahgal's Brush with History," *Probe*, May 1986, p. 17.
2. Doris Lessing, *Going Home* (1957; rpt. St. Albana: Panther, 1977), pp. 41-42.
3. Roy Newquist, "Interview with Doris Lessing," *A Small Personal Voice: Doris Lessing, Essays, Reviews, Interviews,* ed. Paul Schlueter (New York: Vintage, 1975), p. 46.
4. Dutt and Baweja, p. 17.

5. Nayantara Sahgal, "Two Faces of a Novelist," *The Statesman*, 22 August 1970.
6. Nayantara Sahgal, *Prison and Chocolate Cake* (1954; rpt. Bombay: Jaico, 1964), p. 15.
7. Nayantara Sahgal, " Not 'a time to be happy' yet!" *The Tribune*, 13 February 1988, p. 16.
8. Jasbir Jain, *Nayantara Sahgal* (New Delhi: Arnold-Heinemann, 1978), p. 9.
9. Michael Thorpe, *Doris Lessing's Africa* (New York: Holmes and Meier, 1978), p. 104.
10. Mary Ann Singleton, *City and the Veld: The Fiction of Doris Lessing* (Lewisburg: Bucknell University Press, 1977), p. 10: "For Lessing, the African Veld is the unconscious, physical world of nature that nourishes mankind with its unity but also inflicts its own mindless repetition and, in human terms, cruelty and indifference. The city is a half-evolved consciousness, the destructive fragmentation of partial awareness . . . a hope for the future: the unified individual in harmonious society.
11. Florence Howe, "A Conversation with Doris Lessing (1966)," *Contemporary Literature*, 14, No. 4 (Autumn 1973), p. 420.
12. C.J. Driver, "Profile 8: Doris Lessing, " *New Review*, 8, No. 8 (1974), p. 23.
13. Doris Lessing, "Preface," *The Golden Notebook* (1962; rpt, London: Granada, 1983), pp.13-14.
14. Atma Ram, *Interviews with Indo-English Writers* (Calcutta: Writers Workshop, 1983), p. 46.
15. Usha John, "Nayantara Sahgal," *Femina*, 4 Feburary 1972, p. 13.
16. Juliet Mitchell, "Women and Equality," *The Rights and Wrongs of Women*, ed. Juliet Mitchell and Ann Oakley (Harmondsworth: Penguin, 1976), p. 379.
17. Charlotte Bunch, quoted in Lynne Segal, *Is the Future Female? Troubled Thoughts on Contemporary Feminism* (London: Virago, 1987), p. 204.

Feminism

Woman is the chain by which man is attached to the chariot of folly.

Bhartrihari, *Shringar Shatak*

(i) The Subordinate Position of Women

Women are an integral part of human civilization. No society or country can ever progress without an active participation of women in its overall development. Although the place of woman in society has differed from culture to culture and from age to age, yet one fact common to almost all societies is that woman has never been considered the equal of man. Her status largely depends on the simple biological fact that she is the bearer of children whose care is her responsibility; thus her sphere is usually restricted to her familial roles.

Since times immemorial woman has been the victim of male domination and oppression and treated like a beast of burden and an object for pleasure. Man has always looked down upon her as the weaker sex, as his property, servile to him. Different religions of the world have given sanction to the female's subjugation to the male members of society, thus perpetuating the myth of female servitude. *The Bible* clearly tells the women:

> Wives, submit yourselves to your husbands as to the Lord.[1]

Woman is regarded subordinate to man because it is believed that she was made out of man.[2]

In *The Bible* at various places the superiority of man over woman is stressed. Adam is shown as the master who gives names to all beasts and animals, (Genesis 2:20) and he also gives name to his wife and calls her Eve. In the Biblical myth man has been made master of all and he rules over and controls every object on this earth including woman. St. Paul also gives a secondary position to women:

> A man ought not to cover his head, since he is the image and glory of God; but woman is the glory of man.
>
> (I Corinthians 11:7)

He further says:

> Women should be silent during the church meetings. They are not to take part in the discussion, for they are subordinate to men as the scriptures also declare. If they have any questions to ask, let them ask their husbands at home, for it is improper for women to express their opinion in church meetings.
>
> (I Corinthians 14: 34-35)

This concept of women prevalent during the early Christianity affected their status for centuries to come, and the concept of the inferiority of women continued to find expression in such sayings as follows: "as the church is subject to Christ, so let the wives be to their husbands"[3] or "the head of every man is Christ, but the head of woman is man."[4]

The secondary position of women also finds manifestation in the numerical symbolism of Pythagoras who belonged to the sixth century B.C. and whose theory had tremendous impact upon the western culture. According to him, "the number *one* was the number of godhead and of maleness; the number *two* was the number of divisiveness and femaleness. One, God, man, were associated with light, order, good, right, rights, and the right hand. Two, divisiveness or chaos, woman, were associated with darkness, evil, magic, and the sinister, the left hand. To this day, the buttons on men's shirts are on the right, on women's, on the left; to this day, members of a wedding party arrange themselves in a place of worship in accord with these associations: groom's party on the right, bride's party on the left."[5] Significantly, these symbols along with some other conventions still exist and are obeyed in western culture where almost from the moment of birth, the contrast between male and female, rather than their common humanity is stressed, e.g. the baby girls are dressed in pink and baby boys in blue; it seems to be a trifle, but such conventions go a long way in fixing the polarities of the sexes.

Writers, philosophers and thinkers of all ages have striven to show that the subordinate position of women is willed in heaven and advantageous on earth. Jean Jacques Rousseau makes quite damaging statements about women and charges them with capricious nature:

> Women have or ought to have, but little liberty, they are apt to indulge themselves excessively in what is allowed them. Addicted in everything to extremes, they are even more transported at their diversions than boys.[6]

Regarding the purpose of education of women, Rousseau gives this prescription:

> The whole education of women ought to be relative to men. To please them, to be useful to them, to make themselves loved and honoured by them, to educate them when young, to care for them when grown, to counsel them, to make life sweet and agreeable to them – these are the duties of women at all times, and what should be taught them from their infancy.[7]

Even in ancient India, women's lot was no better and they were assigned secondary roles in a male-dominated society by religious injunctions and social conventions. The ancient Hindu law-giver, Manu, whose philosophy occupies a significant place in the mainstream of Indian ideology and culture, does express some noble sentiments about women:

> Where females are honoured, there the deities are pleased; but where they are dishonoured, there all religious acts become fruitless.[8]

Yet, he too constantly stresses the inferiority of women to men. Manu starts with the fundamental principle that all through her existence woman must remain dependent on man:

> In childhood must a female be dependent on her father; in youth, on her husband; her lord being dead, on her sons; if she has no sons, on the near kinsmen of her husband; if she be left no kinsmen, on those of her father; if she has no paternal kinsmen, on the sovereign; a woman must never seek independence. (V, 148)

Verses 14 and 15 of Chapter IX in *Manusmriti* depict women in general as licentious and grossly sensuous; the creator "implanted in them carnal passions, love for ornament, impure desires, wrath, dishonesty, malice and bad conduct." (IX, 17) According to Manu, a wife must ever remain devoted to her husband and always please him while he is alive. After his death she should never think of any other man: "Even though the husband be of bad character and seeks pleasure elsewhere he must be constantly worshipped as a god by a faithful wife." (V, 154) A vicious husband must be worshipped, but a bad wife may at any time be superseded (by another wife). (IX, 80) Elsewhere we read that a wife who has committed faults may be beaten with a rope or a short bamboo. (VIII, 299) Though the widow is strictly enjoined to remain faithful to her husband's memory, there is no corresponding duty on the part of the husband: "After having burnt a wife, who dies before him, the husband may marry again and again." (V, 168) Manu divides Indian society into four *Varnas*: "Brahamans," "Kshatriyas," "Vaishyas" and "Shudras," and the position of women has been equated with the lowest class, Shudras, and like them women are denied various religious privileges. Thus, right in antiquity, double standards were set to determine the roles of men and women.

However, an analysis of the women's status during the Vedic period reveals that they enjoyed a position of equality with men in all spheres. They were given equal opportunities to get education. The goddess of learning is *Saraswati*. Women were eligible for *Upanayana* or initiation and *Brahamacharya* or study of source of knowledge.[9] The *Mahanirvana Tantra* says: "A girl also should be brought up and educated with great effort and care." (8, 47) According to *Saravanukramanika*, there were more than twenty women seers or *brahamvadinis* who composed the hymns of *Rig Veda*, although there is no record of their works. Some writers believe that some of the hymns of *Atharva Veda* were also composed by some women seers. Gargi, Ghosha, Godha, Vishwavara, Apala, Maitreyi, Arundhati and Lilavati were illustrious Vedic women. The *Kaushitaki Brahamana* (7, 6) mentions a learned lady, Pathyaswasti, who travelled all the way to the north to study and obtain the title of "Vach" or the goddess of learning for her scholarship. There is an interesting passage in the *Saptashati* where Durga, who is virgin, tells the Asuras who aspired to marry her: "He who conquers me in battle, he who humbles my pride, he who is my equal in this world, he shall be my husband." Marriage was not compulsory for girls but an unmarried person was not eligible to participate in Vedic sacrifices. Remarriage of widows was allowed and there also prevailed the custom of *Niyoga* according to which a wife could seek extra-marital sex for conceiving a child, in case the husband was incapable of giving her one or had died without giving her one (e.g. the conceptions of the Pandavas, and of Dhritrashtra and Pandu, as described in *Mahabharata*). Women were free to choose their husbands and *Gandharva Vivah* was not uncommon. The freedom of women is evident from the account of the popular festival called *Samanas*, where men and women met and mixed freely. The *Vedas* think of the wife not only as a joint ruler but also as a queen exercising her sovereignty over all the members of the household, including her husband's parents. "The wife, verily, is the home," says the *Veda*. (*Rig Veda*, III, 53.4) Her intellectual personality is recognized and she is invited soon after her marriage to "address the Vidatha" (religious assembly). (*Rig Veda*, X, 85, 26, 27) "The Veda distinguishes itself from all other Indian literature by the high regard in which it holds women."[10]

The vedic age, however, remains an exception in giving equality to women. Yet there too the prayer was always for a boy. *The Atharva Veda* says:

> The birth of a girl, grant it elsewhere,
> here grant a boy. (VI, 23)

This prayer itself is suggestive. In present day India this wish for a boy has assumed inhuman and grotesque proportions and at times leads to female foeticide.

In recent times various anthropological studies and archaeological discoveries have revealed that in the West also women's status was much advanced in ancient civilizations where a state of matriarchy existed and women equally participated in a host of activities like hunting, farming, etc. Many anthropologists believe that "hominids and early humans (*Homo Sapiens*) lived in small groups centered upon the mother; that the millennia fatherhood was unknown."[11] Under different names – Ishtar in Babylon, Astarte in Phoenicia, Cybele in Phrygia, Isis in Egypt – each of the ancient female deities personified the same principle: creation of life, rebirth of nature after the death of winter, hope of resurrection of man. It has also been revealed by the cave paintings and sculpture of these civilizations that certain qualities of great importance like "fertility, regeneration, and a sense of humans as integrally connected with nature"[12] were associated with women. The Earth-Goddess cult, with its belief in the earth as woman, strong and sustaining, began in agricultural societies. Where the Earth-Mother or the Mother-Goddess cult was dominant, maleness was not glorified above femaleness. Women were gradually dislodged from this position of equality by the superior physical strength of men coupled with their desire to ensure that their property was passed on to their rightful heirs.

There are certain matrilineal societies in Kerala in the south and among Garos and Khasis in the north-eastern part of India even today and these provide a qualitatively different social setting for the women in those areas, but they have hardly affected the country's ethos and can be termed only as insignificant exceptions.

The Koran also repeatedly stresses the superiority of men over women. A woman's function in life is to provide the male with sexual gratification and progeny. *The Koran* says:

> Men are superior to women on account of the qualities with which God had gifted the one above the other. . . . Virtuous women are obedient, careful during the husband's absence because God hath on them been careful.[13]

Judaism too did not award equal status to woman in ancient times. She was discriminated against and "never had a franchise – religious, social or political. She was unclean from a religious point of view, and she was nonentity from a political point of view. Beyond ordinary household duties, which she did as a slave or a servant, she was not allowed to share man's work in any walk of life."[14] A Jew made his morning prayer in the following manner:

> Blessed be God . . . that He did not make me a woman.[15]

Buddhism also does not have much to say in favour of women. According to Buddhists, the company of a woman was considered to be an obstacle in the development of higher powers in man. The Buddha tells his disciple:

> Women are soon angered, Ananda,
> Women are full of passion, Ananda,
> Women are envious, Ananda, Women are stupid.
> That is the reason, Ananda, that is the cause,
> Why women have no place in public assemblies, do not carry on business, and do not earn their living by any profession.[16]

Three types of roles were provided to women during this period: housewife, courtesan and nun. Of course, the Buddha made no distinction between a man and a woman regarding the attainment of spiritual ends, and there are many instances of female nuns (*bhikshunis*) attaining perfection, nuns like Mahapajapati Gotami, Kshema, Patachara, Bhadda Kundalakesha, Ambapali, and Vishakha. Yet in the monastic order, the place given to the nuns was lower than that occupied by the monks. There were several restrictions on nuns: "a *bhikshuni*, though of a long standing, must bow before a *bhikshu* ordained much later than her."[17]

Men all over the world have been speaking about women in a derogatory manner. An old Italian saying is: "as a horse, whether good or bad, requires spurs, so a woman whether good or bad, requires thrashing." The wise men of China also advise husbands in these words: "Listen to the counsel of your wife, but act against it." The old men of Russia say: "There is only one soul among ten women." The Spaniards say: "We shall save ourselves from wicked women and should never be captivated by any that have good looks."[18]

In Indian classical literature, a woman is always shown in relationship to man; the husband-wife relationship is given more importance than the daughter-father, sister-brother, or daughter-mother relationship. Traditionally, a "good woman" is always synonymous with good wife and a good wife must be chaste, faithful and virtuous like Sita or Savitri. "For both men and women in Hindu society the ideal woman has been traditionally personified by Sita who is portrayed in the *Ramayana*, as the quintessence of wifely devotion."[19] In *Ramayana*, Sita's identity is solely seen or estimated in relation to her husband, Rama. Her sole purpose in life is to follow in the footsteps of her husband. Sita's image as mother is glorified and she is repeatedly referred to as *Mata Sita*, but as a wife she is subject to the whims of her husband, who abandons her only because of the derogatory remarks of a commoner. However, one finds that Sita shows some sign of awareness of being wronged and refuses to go back to Rama and finally takes refuge in the lap of mother earth.

In scriptures and myths woman is depicted either as a goddess or a sub-human creator, never as a complete human being. Where on one hand, she has been described as an object of reverence or worship, on the other hand, she is treated like an object of sexual gratification and considered to be man's property. In every age, the recurrent symbol of seed and earth further degrades her position. "Man provides the seed, the essence for the creation of the offspring; the seed determines the kind; the child's identity is derived from the father for the group placement. The role of the mother is just to receive the seed and through her own blood provide warmth and nourishment and help it to grow."[20]

Apart from the religio-cultural factors, the historical and political events also appear to have had their impact on the status of women in ancient India. Due to the repeated invasions by foreign rulers, woman lost the honour and respect earlier commanded by her in the Vedic society. Sons were valued more than the daughters as they could participate in wars because ancient civilizations were constantly exposed to such dangers.[21]

Later, because of the impact of Islamic culture, the "Purdah system" came into being, which further secluded women from the society. Sati system, child marriage, ban on widow-marriage are some of the evils added during different ages which further lowered the status of women in Indian society.

There is a great discrepancy between the idealized concept of woman in Indian myths and scriptures and her actual situation in life. On the surface she enjoys a very high status and is known as *Devi* (Goddess), *Lakshmi* (Goddess of wealth), or *Shakti* (Goddess of power), but in real life she is harassed, oppressed and tortured in various ways. Female infanticide, *sati*, harassment of widows, rape, wife battering, family violence, dowry deaths in recent times are some of the visible forms of the oppression on women. One recalls the observation made by a leading sociologist who said that even "the poorest Indian male is fortunate in having opportunities for releasing his impulse to domination and the fury of his frustrated ego, because he always has a wife whom he can treat as an inferior."[22] The complete self-effacement or total submission on the part of a woman is considered to be the highest virtue. Traditionally, her destiny is marriage, and as a married woman, she must be a *Pativrata* and worship her husband like a God because by serving him only a woman can reach *Swarga* (Heaven).

In the Directive Principles of State in the Constitution of free India, sufficient legal and constitutional security has been ensured to women. The passing of certain acts like "The Termination of Pregnancy Act," "The Maternity Benefit Act" and "The Dowry Prohibition Act" has brought some measure of relief to women of all castes, creeds and religions. A greater awareness and expression of women's problems are coming to the fore through the press and other media.

A feminist publishing house, "Kali for Women," is engaged in publishing books on women by women. A number of feminist journals like *Samya Shakti* or *Manushi* have also started appearing in India. Some film producers have focused on women's problems and have produced art films in which women have been shown asserting their individuality and independence, though such films are patronized by only a small section of the society.

Despite the spread of education and some constitutional gains, the subordination of women preached by religion and perpetuated by conventions is the rule of the day. Social structures and cultural norms do not change as rapidly as laws envisage. The performance of *Sati* (self-immolation of a widow) by Roop Kanwar of Deorala village in Rajasthan in September 1987 points to the age-old prejudices women are still subjected to. Though the evil practice of Sati, which was very popular among Rajputs in India during the seventeenth and eighteenth centuries, was abolished by Lord William Bentick, yet this recent incident of Sati is indicative of the still-prevalent patriarchal belief that a married woman's existence comes to an end after her husband's death. The glorification of Roop Kanwar's act (which was probably forced on her) in Chunari ceremony in which thousands of people participated is a sad index of how ineffective law is.

In the past, for unwanted female babies, female infanticide was in practice; today it is female foeticide. Depression of girls at the sex-discrimination by the parents can be measured from the act of triple suicide by three sisters in Chandigarh on 9th March, 1989 soon after their parents were blessed with a son. The desire for a son can make the parents ignore their bright, talented grown-up daughters resulting in catastrophe.

The media are also responsible for projecting the image of women in a distorted manner. In the TV or newspaper advertisements, women are portrayed as sexy, glamorous and empty-headed. Indian films, too, preach feminine values of submission, devotion and self-sacrifice. The attitude of the press towards distressed women is rather unhealthy and quite unsympathetic, and often presents cases of rape, etc. as spicy stories.

With the exception of some gains in education and employment for middle-class women, the women's position in practice is still very bad. Even the economically independent woman's lot is no better. She has to bear the double burden – of job and household responsibilities. At home her contribution is seldom recognized while at her working place many times she is treated as inferior or is harassed and exploited. Among the cases of dowry deaths, rape and sexual harassment, not infrequently, the educated working women are the victims. In the lower paid jobs women work for longer hours and still also bear full responsibility for the household work. The rural women, apart from looking after family and children, also work the whole day in fields, but instead of any word of gratitude they are slighted by various members of the family and are often victims of physical violence as well. Economically the middle-class working women may not face hardships like their counterparts in the lower classes, still they are dependent on men, who may or may not provide them with necessary comforts. But within the family, they do not have satisfying relationships as their individuality is never recognized or cared for. They are again subject to the whims of other members of the family, husband or children, whose happiness is supposed to be the sole purpose of the woman's life. Even in America, where women are supposed to be more liberated, they suffer sexual harassment from their superiors in offices, etc.[23] Such cases are not rare, but remain unknown as the victims quietly bear harassment out of the fear of social disgrace.

(ii) Heading towards Women's Emancipation

An increasing awareness of injustice done to them slowly made women raise their voice against inequality and oppression and in the twentieth century this female consciousness against male domination led to the birth of women's liberation movement which is a serious reform movement aiming at an upliftment of women in society. The first voice in favour of women's rights was in fact raised much earlier. The first major feminist manifesto *A Vindication of the Rights of Women* published in 1792 was written by Mary Wollstonecraft, who demanded equal opportunities for women in the field of education, economics and politics. An attack on the social and economic systems, *A Vindication* strongly pleaded for women's education and their protection by laws. In her introduction to *A Vindication* Wollstonecraft demands that women should be treated as human beings:

> Dismissing, then, those pretty feminine phrases, which the men condescendingly use to soften our slavish dependence, and despising that weak elegancy of mind, exquisite sensibility, and sweet docility of manners, supposed to be the sexual characteristics of the weaker vessel, I wish to show that elegance is inferior to virtue, that the first object of laudable ambition is to obtain a character as a human being, regardless of the distinction of sex, and that secondary views should be brought to this simple touchstone.[24]

Wollstonecraft argues that the principles and attitudes which suggest that woman "was created to be the toy of man, his rattle, and it must jingle in his ears whenever, dismissing reasons, he chooses to be amused,"[25] must be repudiated before a real change in her condition could be gained permanently. She strongly condemns the religious attitude which is also responsible for giving secondary position to women. She regrets that "taught from their infancy that beauty is woman's sceptre, the mind shapes itself to the body, and roaming round its gilt cage, only seeks to adore its prison."[26] Thus *A Vindication* is the first document where the full humanity of women is asserted and the author insists upon its recognition. Even today when a certain amount of educational and political freedom has been attained, the recognition and acceptance of women as independent, individual human beings, having their own independent personality, remains the crucial issue. In fact, what modern feminists are demanding is an echo of what is already demanded in *A Vindication*. As far back as 1697 Mary Astell had raised her voice for education of women, yet none could see women's problems and raise voice in their favour so completely as Mary Wollstonecraft.

In eighteenth century William Blackstone, a distinguished professor of law at Oxford, described marriage as a "civil death" of woman. In his *Commentaries on the English Constitution* (1758) and *Commentaries on the Laws of England*, he states:

> By marriage, the husband and wife are one person in law; that is, the very being or legal existence of the woman is suspended during the marriage, or at least is incorporated and consolidated into that of the husband: under whose wing, protection and cover she performs everything.[27]

One of the strong male supporters of women's cause was John Stuart Mill who in his *The Subjection of Women* (1869) showed serious concern over some of the issues earlier raised by Wollstonecraft. Like her he also felt the need for improved education for women in all spheres and said that the power of earning is essential to the dignity of women. A true democrat and a champion of freedom, Mill fought for liberty and individual freedom. He believed that women's oppression was because of the system and condemned it as "domestic slavery." He condemned the attitudes which regulated the existing social relations between the two sexes, the legal subordination of one sex to the other and considered it the chief hindrance to human improvement.

In the Victorian England, some women writers also wrote articles on women's problems but they were not given enough attention. For example, Harriet Martineau (1802-76), a contemporary of Elizabeth Barrett and Charlotte Bronte, was a serious feminist. Her feminist writings are scattered through magazines, newspapers and periodicals. She made a plea for better education for girls in *Society in America* (1837) and *Household Education* (1849). She echoes Wollstonecraft when she pleads that women should be educated to their fullest capacities and they should be taught to think. She thought women's lot resembled that of a slave. Martineau often wrote about the problems of working women and discriminatory treatment meted out to them, and about women in prison and problems of women with "violent husbands."[28]

In 1848, Queen's College, the first women's college in England, was set up for imparting better education to girls for their better prospects. So far as imparting education to women was concerned, it was quite satisfactory, but except for teaching, there were no other dignified professions open to women. Education infused necessary confidence in women and soon a large number of women entered many fields of social service like working for prison reforms, fighting alcoholism, cruelty to children, campaigning against slavery and also fought for feminine causes like reforms in marriage and divorce laws. The next step was asking for political freedom. Gradually, several countries granted political rights to women. The first countries to grant women electoral equality with men were New Zealand (1893), Finland (1906), Norway (1913), Denmark and Iceland (1915), Soviet Union (1917), U.S.A. (1920), and Britain (1928). Suffrage was granted to women in many other countries of the world after World War I or in the wake of World War II. It was in the sixties that the feminist movement took the shape of a revolution.

The earliest wave of American Feminism emerged in 1800, during the period of industrial development, which "provided the context for the first collective assault on traditional ideas about women's place"[29] when women demanded equality in various spheres. Its efforts were towards expansion of educational opportunities to women. In 1833, Oberline College was the first to admit women students. In 1830s together with men, women protested in large numbers for the abolition of slavery. In 1848 at Seneca Falls, New York, a large number of men and women gathered to issue a "Declaration of Sentiments" and challenged the traditional framework of woman's place. They demanded that women should also have the right to individual development, educationally and politically and fought for it in assemblies.

Despite all these efforts and achievements, the traditional attitudes towards woman's "place" continued to affect woman's position adversely. For the same work, women were paid less as it was alleged that women worked only to secure extra cash for frivolous purchases. Many magazines publicised the "cult of domesticity" and instructed women to be "modest, meek, obedient and pious – qualities nearly identical with the piety, purity, submissiveness and domesticity."[30] With the passage of time, many new virtues were being included in the list, viz., youth, appearance and acquiescence.

During the colonial rule in India, there was an awareness of the need of improvement in women's condition, and the idea to impart education to women was revived. For this purpose several missionary schools and later girl's colleges were opened in various parts of the country. Further, the birth of two movements, i.e. Social Reform Movement and Nationalist Movement during the nineteenth century, had deep impact on the status of women.

The issues which attracted the attention of social reformers like Raja Rammohan Roy, Dayanand Saraswati, Ishwar Chander Vidyasagar were Sati, ill-treatment of widows, illiteracy of women, etc. They thought that by giving women access to education and by enacting progressive legislation, social change could be initiated. They believed in reviving the old Vedic society which promised equal status to women.

The Indian National Movement under the leadership of Mahatma Gandhi led to further emancipation of Indian women in the twentieth century by involving them in the struggle for political freedom of the country. Gandhiji vehemently criticized the customs of child marriage, prohibition on widow remarriage, temple prostitution and the custom of purdah. He had deep faith in women's inner strength and in his various Satyagraha movements vast numbers of women participated. Inspired and encouraged by men, a host of women also organized themselves under noted personalities like Pandita Ramabai, Ramabai Ranade and Anandibai Joshi for the betterment of their kind and to struggle against the heavy odds.

With the growth of educational and vocational opportunities, the educated middle and upper-class women, particularly in urban areas, are becoming conscious of their rights. To quote Rajkumari Amrit Kaur, "We are aware of the necessity of finding and being judged by our own standards as free human beings, voluntarily accepted; we are determined to face the facts of life, to fight the battle of our sex and take the risk."[31]

The formation of All India Women's Conference in 1927 was a crucial event in this regard. The A.I.W.C. has been instrumental in bringing about some reforms like the Sharda Act (1929) banning child marriage, the Dissolution of the Muslim Marriage Act (1939) and the bill for better supervision of orphanages, rescue homes and marriage bureaus (1940). There are more than 2500 agencies in the country working for women and children. Some of these groups and agencies have succeeded in campaigning against rape and sexual molestation and also brought about national debate on these subjects.[32] While some groups work more like only consciousness-raising groups, other groups actively help women in distress by providing shelter to helpless women or creating channels for professional activity. Some groups are involved in research and documentation on women's issues and both educationists and activists are members of such groups.

The Women's Liberation Movement in India, mainly functioning on the social and economic level, is largely concerned with issues like atrocities against women, wife-beating, rape, dowry-deaths, alcoholism, violence in the family, problems of working women, traffic in women, personal laws and health issues.

From the early nineteenth century to the 1950s, women's movement remained a marginal movement in the West. In 1953 the English translation of French writer Simone de Beauvoir's *Le Deuxieme Sexe* (written in 1949) appeared, which proved a major influence on the women liberation movement. Simone de Beauvoir is a radical feminist, belonging to the first generation of new feminists. In *The Second Sex* she draws heavily on the disciplines of biology, psychoanalysis, political economy, anthropology, philosophy and history. She studies in detail issues like a girl's education, female sexuality, marriage, prostitution and house-work which she calls unrewarding drudgery. Her own life and her companionship with Jean Paul Sartre seemed a model for independent women. She met Sartre at Sorbonne when both were in their twenties and lived together without marrying till death.

The chief argument of de Beauvoir's book is that in patriarchy women have been forced to occupy a secondary position in relation to men, a position comparable in many respects to that of racial minorities in spite of the fact that they constitute at least one half of the human race. She believes that this secondary position is not imposed of necessity by natural "feminine" characteristics but rather by strong environmental forces of social traditions and education which have been under the control of men. This has resulted in the failure of women to take a place of human dignity as free and independent existents. This has not only limited their achievements in many fields but has also given rise to pervasive social evils and has had a particularly vitiating effect on the sexual relations between men and women. Man considers himself Subject and Absolute and woman is the Other:

> She is called "the sex," by which is meant that she appears essentially to the male as a sexual being. For him she is sex – absolute sex, no less . . . she is the incidental, the inessential as opposed to the essential. He is the Subject, he is the Absolute – she is the Other.[33]

Man always thinks that he is in the right, while woman is in the wrong; all the negative qualities are assigned to her. He is afraid of feminine competition. The position of women is changing steadily and they are beginning to take part in the affairs of the world also but it is "still a world that belongs to men" (21); the subjugation of women continues and thus "we are exhorted to be women, remain women, become women." (13) Man's function is living life, and his place is in the world and woman's is in the home. She has been treated as a beast of luxury (coquettes and courtesans), beasts of burden (harried housewives) or as the devil's handmaiden. Man either sees her as a source of transcendence or projects his own guilt on her. Deliver her from the myth of the Eternal Female and let her create herself, i.e. put woman in an existential perspective. She can transcend her subservient position only by having some activity of her own.

While in the first part of her book, "Facts and Myths," de Beauvoir makes a study of sexism in the works of some selected authors, in the second part, "Woman's Life Today," she deals with the matter of woman's education. Woman is trained to think of herself as inferior. De Beauvoir says that the books she read in her childhood depicting men as heroes and women as victims and later she read classical plays and novels – all these perpetuated the myths of Eternal Female. These books teach woman how to be seductive and how to win husbands. De Beauvoir argues that for emancipation women must seek professional autonomy and financial independence and also avoid marriage and children.

De Beauvoir frankly discusses taboo-ridden topics like sexual initiation, sexual pleasure for women. She says that woman is not a free agent in choosing the man of her erotic destiny, and her desires and pleasures are at the mercy of an institution and for a long time she has been denied the right to pleasure. Man is never consistent; he wants his wife to be passionate but indifferent to men as a whole. He wants her to be entirely his. Thus, she is betrayed from the day he marries her. Bound to one man, with children to tend, woman's life is over. She finds no future outside of her husband's. De Beauvoir asserts that the bond between man and woman should be based on common love and consent. She also deals with the issues of unwanted motherhood, the unmarried mother and abortion. In contrast to the prevailing sentimental propaganda about maternity, de Beauvoir described maternity with disgust and it came to many women as a welcome revelation.

Simone de Beauvoir concludes that women should be freed from the bonds of slavery. Despite the myths, women are not weak; nor is there eternal hostility between the sexes. She finds sharing the only solution to the problems of man-woman relationship.

After so many years of its publication, the book still continues to exercise a significant influence on the feminist literature. However, in 1953 when the English translation of the book appeared, it did not initiate any movement as it happened in 1963 when the women's government took the shape of a revolution with the publication of Betty Friedan's *The Feminine Mystique*.

The Feminine Mystique took the American society by storm. Feminism as it now exists dates from the publication of this book, which had a tremendous impact on society. Based mainly on interviews with the Friedan's classmates, fifteen years after graduation from a woman's college, the book challenges the popular belief that a woman's place is at her home and that she should find fulfilment in motherhood and domesticity, which had religiously been perpetuated all through the ages. Defining the "feminine mystique" or the "incommunicable quality," she writes in the preface:

> There was a strange discrepancy between the reality of our lives as women and the image to which we were trying to conform, the image that I came to call the feminine mystique.[34]

Most of the women whom Friedan interviewed were married, had comfortable homes, children and were blessed with all the comforts of life, yet they conformed to the image of Friedan's "feminine mystique." They had no purpose in their lives and were faithfully playing their role of devoted wife and loving mother and were supposed to seek fulfilment in it. But this in fact created a sense of "emptiness, non-existence and nothingness" (264) in them. Friedan accuses society for not permitting women to gratify their basic needs of self-fulfilment to grow and fulfil their potential as human beings. Seeking an independent identity is considered only the male's privilege. The core problem for women is not sex but identity which has always been denied to them. Friedan says that a woman can never ask questions like "Who am I? What do I want?" But now for the first time women are becoming aware of this identity crisis which began much earlier. Friedan also rejects Freud's opinion about women that they can glory only in their own femininity.

Friedan finally declares that "for woman, as for man, the need for self-fulfilment – autonomy, self-realization, independence, individuality, self-actualization – is as important as the sexual need, with as serious consequences, when it is thwarted. Woman's sexual problems are, in this sense, by-products of the suppression of her basic need to grow and fulfil her potentialities as a human being, potentialities which the mystique of feminine fulfilment ignores." (282) She further argues that a woman can find fulfilment only in a creative work of her own. Friedan, however, did not discard the institution of marriage as the militant feminists later did.

Another important feminist of the twentieth century is Kate Millett who, in her book *Sexual Politics* (1969), impressively marshalled the historical argument for feminism that women ought to be given equal treatment in society. She describes the relation between the sexes as basically political. It is an arrangement "whereby one group of persons is controlled by another."[35] She argues that for the establishment of patriarchal society, the status accorded to women has been a demeaning one, that of the homemaker and chattel, and feels that all but rudimentary sexual differences are cultural in origin.

The book includes sympathetic discussion of Frederick Engels's *The Origin of the Family, Private Property and the State* (1884). Engels believed that among primitive tribes, both men and women participated in occupations equally for the good of their community, but with the beginning of trade arose the concept of private property and the desire to bequeath it to one's own sons. And this led to the subjugation of women, as woman because of her capacity to reproduce was considered a property. Millett believes that patriarchy imposed strict fidelity and subservience on women. Millett also hopes for the times when the monogamous family will cease to exist and when the raising of offspring will be left to trained practitioners of both sexes, instead of parents. Like other militant feminists, she also discourages small family consisting of parents and children. She, too, condemns Freud's theory of "penis envy" and his contribution to psychoanalytic thought, his attitude towards women in particular. Millett thinks that one of the aims of freeing women is to free them from "immemorial subordination" which in the process can bring us " a great deal closer to humanity." (363)

In her book, *The Female Eunuch* (1970), Germaine Greer suggests that "women ought not to enter into socially sanctioned relationship, like marriage"[36] because "If women are to effect a significant amelioration in their condition it seems obvious that they must refuse to marry." (319) Greer, like Kate Millett regards the small nuclear family as a disaster and would like children to be reared by many willing adults, not necessarily their biological parents. This change would release children from the disadvantage of being extensions of their parents so that they can belong primarily to themselves.

Beginning with suffragettes who Greer thinks have failed to achieve emancipation she comes to various liberation movements organized in 1970s, and condemns the women politicians who try to represent interests of "women as dependants." (12) Separating earlier reformers from the latter, she differentiates their aims: earlier, "genteel middle-class ladies clamoured for reform, now ungenteel middle-class women are calling for revolution." (11)

To study man-woman relationship, Greer uses the analogy of employer and employee and calls women "life-contracted unpaid workers" (329) who cannot expect liberation "unless individual women agree to be outcasts, eccentrics, perverts, and whatever the powers-that-be choose to call them." (328) She tells women that "to be emancipated from the helplessness and need and walk freely upon the earth that is your birthright," (330) they have to fight for it.

Challenged in a television interview about the meaning of this book's title, Greer replied it was not she, "but Freud, who said women were castrated, hence eunuch. The aim of her work is to restore to women their uncastrated feminity."[37]

During 1970, a group of radical feminists advocated their theories of equality. In this period, Shulamith Firestone's *The Dialectic of Sex* (1970), Eva Figes's *Patriarchal Attitudes* (1970), Mitchell's *Women's Estate* (1971), and Ann Oakley's *Sex, Gender and Society* (1972), *The Sociology of Housework* (1974), *Housewife* (1976) appeared. Defining radical feminism, Shulamith Firestone observes:

> In the radical feminist view, the new feminism is not just the revival of a serious political movement for social equality. It is the second wave of the most important revolution in history. Its aim: overthrow of the oldest, most rigid class/caste system in existence, the class system based on sex—a system consolidated over the thousands of years, lending archetypal male and female roles an undeserved sexual legitimacy and seeming permanence. The Western feminist movement is the dawn of a long struggle to break free from the oppressive power structure set up by Nature and reinforced by men.[38]

These feminists reject any kind of discrimination on the basis of sex and declare in the epigraph of one of the books on the subject:

> The fault lies not in our stars, our harmones, our menstrual cycles or our empty internal spaces but in our institutions—Woman is made, not born.[39]

Women's oppression is traced not to individual male malevolence but to the social and familial structures based on patriarchy. The problem as identified was that a woman's identity was expected to be merged with, and grow from her role as wife and mother; female children grew up with indoctrination that held up, overtly and covertly, this ideal as the only one a "good" woman was to aspire for; and they believed that it was this cultural conditioning that was the culprit, not any inherent biological difference. Hence, women were urged to fight such conditioning by attaining positions of power and prestige and by eliminating gender differences because ultimately, as Sheila Rowbotham suggests, "the liberation of women necessitates the liberation of all human beings."[40]

There are certain differences in the ideological viewpoints among the various groups of feminists. While the more radical group rejects outright the institution of marriage and considers it as an organized rape, the less militant feminists like Betty Friedan want to seek fulfilment within marriage itself, but oppose nuclear family system. However, during the "war of the sexes" (to use the words of James Thurber, an American humanist) the members of the radical group in the process of "consciousness-raising" rituals came together against men and confided to women of the group their adverse experiences at the hands of men. They also evolved a new vocabulary, viz., "consciousness raising" (making women conscious of their subordinate position to men in the society and questioning this subordination), "male chauvinism" (the assumption that male needs and capabilities are superior to those of women), "sexist" (to prejudge role by gender), "sex-object" (a woman seen primarily in terms of sexual attractiveness to men), "full humanity" (a full human being). An American feminist Gloria Steinem publicized "Ms." a new "liberated" form of address which avoids identifying women on the basis of their marital status. These radical feminists, apart from demanding equal educational and career opportunities, also advocated a drastic reorganization of society and gender roles. They threatened a revolution which would overthrow the dominance of one half of the world's population over the other on the basis of sex. And for that purpose they wanted that women should be united to achieve self-reliance, self-sufficiency and self-respect and together they should fight for this cause and not aspire for favours from men. Thus, the concept of "sisterhood" was born which means women must develop friendship and assert their identification with one another. In a patriarchal society, they have been separated from each other. They want to unite all women – Black or White, working or non-working, of lower- or middle-class. But, as Juliet Mitchell and Ann Oakley explain, the "concept of sisterhood means much more than sharing work or responsibility. It involves a redefinition of the value and status of personal experience. The personal becomes the political; that is, the nature of women's oppression can be analyzed through the medium of accounts of private experiences."[41]

The radicals further made an extreme demand to "abolish all differences in dress and demeanor, personal adornment, sexual initiative and the allocation of homemaking and parental duties,"[42] and wanted to lead "the androgynous life" to save themselves from time-wasting frivolity and petty narcissism.

The aim of different groups of feminists is the same, i.e. to liberate women from male oppression and to promote women's rights. But the radicals further suggest that woman must not be a slave to her biological functions. Child bearing must be voluntary, and hence, woman must have the right to have abortion on demand. The state must treat abortion at par with other forms of medical care so that a poor woman is not denied abortion if she cannot afford to pay the exorbitant rates. Feminists condemn prostitution and rape and advise their sisters to learn to defend themselves against it. The radical feminists do not want to work politically with men or in "male organizations."

In fact, feminists want a humanist and unprejudiced attitude towards women. Though there are different strands of thought within feminism, all of them see women as a distinct and oppressed social group. They may use different vocabularies and concepts, but their analysis of women's problems is essentially the same. All of them believe that breaking down male and female stereotypes and giving women equality is the only way to a better world. As Angela Weir and Elizabeth Wilson observe, women's liberation is an "Umbrella movement, a 'broad church' that could accommodate every kind of feminism."[43]

Among the many groups of women's movement is a less popular group known as "Bourgeois Feminism" which became known during the mid-twentieth century. Bourgeois Feminism has been defined by Juliet Mitchell:

> "Bourgeois Feminism" in the mid-twentieth century must indicate a tendency within the women's movement that believes that its demand can be met within the context of the present capitalist society.[44]

Socialist feminists hold that women's inferior status is rooted in private property and class-divided society. They find it necessary to understand the operation of hierarchical sexual ordering of the society within the class structure. They feel that overthrow of the capitalist system by itself will not mean a transformation of the patriarchal ideology. It would be necessary to organize struggles simultaneously against capitalism and patriarchy. According to socialist feminists, the powerlessness of women in society is rooted in four basic structures: those of production, reproduction, sexuality and socialization of children. Family is an institution which reinforces women's oppressive condition. The unequal and hierarchical sex roles operate in the domain of both family and economy.

The socialist feminists do not believe in the primacy of male powers but believe that the subordination of woman arose "as a result of capitalism."[45] Hence, the socialist feminists cannot "accept the divorce of women's oppression from all other oppressions... in a class society, and faced with the global aggression of imperialist capitalism and the existence of national liberation struggles, women had to form alliances with other exploited and oppressed groups to free themselves and their sisters."[46]

The socialists emphasize the primacy of social and economic system while the radicals explain even social and economic exploitation in terms of male dominance. Women get identified with all sorts of marginalized groups. Woman has been equated with unprivileged groups like blacks or slaves and her *position* sidelined or "marginalized by the patriarchal symbolic order"[47] in the society. Feminists strongly resent this "border-line" position of women and feel it necessary "to defend women *as* women in order to counteract the patriarchal oppression that precisely despises women *as* women."[48]

In the West, especially in Britain during the 1980s, coloured women formed their own group known as "Black Feminists." They criticized the radical group which they alleged was dominated by white women and called them racists. While for the earlier feminists sexual emancipation was taboo, the modern feminists discuss female sexuality openly and believe that women are not merely vessels of male sexual gratification. Woman too can enjoy biological function and give it some meaning in her emotional and physical life. In their desire to assert their independence and revolt against male sexual tyranny, they are turning towards lesbianism as a solution to the problems of heterosexual relationships.

In the eighties, certain feminists have postulated new theories on feminism in which they have changed their earlier radical stand and have taken a fresh view of the women's problems. For these feminists, equality does not mean a rejection of femaleness. They seek rights within the existing social and familial patterns. Two decades after *The Feminine Mystique*, Betty Friedan now states in her *The Second Stage* (1981) that humanity can only survive if women make certain compromises. Her argument is that women have changed, family patterns have changed, sexual norms have shifted, and the institutions must also change to accommodate present reality in order to survive. It requires not only a shift in women's consciousness, but a flexibility that will allow institutions to absorb present experience without de-stabilizing themselves. It means evolving new forms of living within the changing context of the American family. If in the first stage women were involved in breaking the stranglehold of the feminine mystique, she writes in the "second stage" it is the feminist mystique that must be laid aside. "Improbable as it may seem, we could bridge the old conservative liberal chasm, if we realize the true potential of that elusive new male-female, second-stage mode."[49] Here, she adopts a new vision of the family. The emphasis is on women abandoning their rage, their "strident" anti-family and anti-male position and going back to the family, which she stresses, has always been the source of women's power. Free from the constriction of the feminism mystique, women can re-embrace the institution. Women, she writes, need to cherish the more human labour of nurture and the security of close relationships because these are women's real needs. "We are beginning to be afraid because the cycle we broke and have to re-embrace again is basic to life." (36) She admits that "it may sound corny, but there is a power in women's ability to create life, closeness to life, that men don't have." (161)

Marilyn French, better known for her novels, *The Women's Room* (1978) and *The Bleeding Heart* (1980), in her feminist text *Beyond Power: On Women, Men and Morals* (1986) expresses similar views in a different garb. She defines feminism as "a political movement demanding access to the rewards and responsibilities of the 'male' world, but it is more: it is a revolutionary moral movement, intending to use political power to transform society, to 'feminize' it."[50] She argues that unless we embrace alternative human and humane values which have been considered feminine, we are heading towards a totalitarian world. She is convinced that only feminism with its vision of a new morality can restore harmony to life. Marilyn French investigates the nature and effects of power and calls on a number of disciplines (history, anthropology, political theory, medicine and law) to demonstrate that patriarchy is neither natural nor inevitable and that, in fact, no model exists for it. She says ancient matriarchies with their emphasis on nurture and sharing were overthrown by a male ideology which sought to control nature and achieve transcendence over earthly life. Women were identified with nature and for 5000 years, patriarchy suppressed women and worshipped power and controlled every essence of nature and brought the world on the brink of extinction.

The quintessence of her argument is that only when men influenced by the values of feminism replace power with pleasure, competitiveness with cooperation, individualism with community and transcendence with the joys of living and reorder their priorities accordingly can the world really change.

The Australian born "apocalyptic" feminist Lynne Segal also puts forth a similar argument in her study *Is the Future Female? Troubled Thoughts on Contemporary Feminism* (1987). She challenges the feminist orthodoxies on marriage, motherhood and female sexuality. She argues that in order to understand and alter the power relations between men and women, we must look at the diverse patterns of domination and exploitation in the home, at work, and in our cultural and political lives, and work out strategies to forge a new future for women and men. Like Marilyn French she also suggests that to save the world from destruction feminine values should be given equal significance along with masculine values.

Apart from raising crucial issues, the feminists aim at bringing about a moral revolution for the betterment of the world, and seek more meaningful relationships based on trust and companionship rather than on power politics where one sex dominates the other.

(iii) Feminist Literature and Feminist Literary Criticism

Feminist literature can in fact be a significant instrument in foregrounding the feminine values. In feminist literature woman's experience becomes the central concern. This literature seeks to demythologize the myth that man is the universal representative of humanity, and woman is the unnamed and the invisible. Hence, the need for women writers to write their own literature which provides centrality to woman in every way – thematically, structurally and stylistically.

Long before the advent of women's liberation movement many writers talked about the oppressive conditions of women in the male-dominated society. In nineteenth century in particular we find that women writers like Jane Austen, Charlotte Bronte, Mrs. Gaskell, Dorothy Richardson, George Eliot, Virginia Woolf and Margaret Drabble anticipated some of the present-day feminist issues in their respective works. In twentieth century, a more conscious and articulate attempt has been made by the women to speak for themselves and of the areas of experience related to themselves. And then followed attempts to find their own images, symbols, form and syntax. Dorothy Richardson was perhaps the first to feel the need. In *Pilgrimage* she was trying to create what she termed the "Feminist prose." Stating her purpose in the "Preface," she said that hers was an attempt to produce a feminine equivalent to the current masculine realism. She suggested that feminist prose should be unpunctuated, moving from point to point without formal obstruction.

Virginia Woolf's contribution to literature from the feminist angle is certainly very significant. She felt that literature is a cultural product which can be challenged and changed to open up new possibilities for women and give them a voice. Women felt the need to express emotions and feelings rather than actions in their works. Writing about the difference in male and female experience and its expression in literature, Virginia Woolf wrote:

> There is the obvious and enormous difference of experience in the first place; but the essential difference lies in the fact not that men describe

> battles and women the birth of children, but that each sex describes itself.[51]

To achieve new possibilities, she felt the need to break down the limits and norms of traditional literature. She wanted to write and be read as a woman not merely as a "surrogate" man. She was in search of "feminine identity in literature and a feminine style,"[52] as Suzanne Hall puts it. Woolf wanted a feminine prose or a "woman's sentence" free from the limitations of punctuation and grammar—a style more mobile and flexible to express female experience. Woman's prose or syntax is a challenge to the authority of the so-called grammatically correct sentence. This tradition of extraordinary experiment with language has been carried on by many women writers including Doris Lessing.

Some critics like Elaine Showalter recommend that women writers should develop a "vocabulary for the body" to describe the female sexual behaviour uninhibitedly, which would also provide an alternative to the misogynistic male sexual language. Doris Lessing does describe the female sexual experience and other taboo subjects with amazing candour (in *The Golden Notebook*) which can be almost shocking for an average male reader.

In the feminist literature male language has been countered by the creation of a different kind of language, one that is more expressive, more personal and lays more stress on body. Critics have analyzed the language spoken by men and the language spoken by women and found some inherent differences, for example, the speech of the women is more hesitant, less fluent and the sentences are left unfinished. Also, women are more silent, interrupt less frequently, use tag questions; cooperative strategies are preferred to competitiveness. Women, in short, tend to adopt a more socially-oriented and submissive pattern of behaviour than men. This, however, does not indicate, as critics like Robin Lakoff and others suggest, that women are diffident, timid or unsure of themselves; rather as Marilyn French maintains,[53] their style is indicative of their desire for sharing, for communication, for interaction and for harmony. Their sentence is in direct contrast to a male sentence that ends with a snapping finality, barring all possibility of interaction.

All these strategies, i.e. finding their own subject matter—their own bodies, their own emotions, their own responses to the world—and their own style are, in fact, an attempt on women's part to find a place for themselves. Sandra M. Gilbert says that "woman must inevitably find that she has no home, no where," and that there is a sense of metaphysical alienation, "I look for myself through the centuries and don't see myself anywhere."[54] Her words echo those of Elizabeth Barrett Browning: "I look everywhere for grandmothers and find none."[55]

As a result of the feminist movement of the sixties, a new approach to study literature evolved known as feminist literary criticism or Woman's Studies movement. The earliest attempt was certainly Kate Millett's who in her *Sexual Politics* argued that women are politically and socially oppressed by a patriarchal system that uses sex for purposes of domination; and showed how this ideology is present in the works of D.H. Lawrence, Henry Miller, Norman Mailer, and Jean Genet. There was an outpour of books on feminist literary criticism in the seventies and it continues till today. New journals were started expressing a feminist point of view, such as *Signs: A Journal of Women in Culture and Society* (University of Chicago Press, 1975), *International Journal of Women's Studies* (Eden Press, 1978), *Journal of Women's Studies in Literature* (1978), *Feminist Studies* (University of Maryland, 1973), *Women's Studies: An Interdisciplinary Journal* (Queens College, 1972). Special numbers of various other journals on feminist studies keep on appearing. Women's Studies have been included in higher education not only in countries like the United States and England but also in India. Some universities have introduced Departments of Women Studies separately while others have included courses on Women's Studies in the existing syllabi. In 1988 UGC directed seven universities to prepare draft syallabi on women's studies for incorporation in the undergraduate programme as well.[56]

The feminist literary criticism studies literature in the light of its ideology. It analyzes literary texts to see the role and position of women in them. And the feminist critics find that woman is often "marginalized," "repressed" or "silenced" in literary works. Hence, feminist criticism seeks to reinterpret the works of earlier authors of both sexes in order to expose misconceptions and culturally conditioned responses. Feminist criticism is committed. It is a specific kind of political discourse which takes a stand against patriarchy and sexism. Its objectives are social and cultural. Like the Marxist critic, it sees literature as the product of a particular society and does not believe that literature is a purely "aesthetic construct" divorced from social reality. Feminist criticism takes literature seriously as a criticism of life. It rejects the premise that male experience is the universal norm, and refuses to see the female experience as "peripheral."

Cheri Register described some of the aims of the feminist critics as follows:

> We would challenge critics's claims of objectivity and their belief in the neutrality of literature as aesthetic construct. We would expose the misogynistic stereotyping of women in the classics. We would rescue female writers from oblivion and get them into the canon.[57]

Stereotyping results from the basic idea of identifying "the fully human with the male – to see women as flat embodiments of a particular force or theme, to see them mythically, allegorically, symbolically but never realistically, as fully rounded complex human beings."[58] Feminist critics are highly critical of the stereotype images of woman as "temptress," because this stereotyping is a product of social conditioning and fulfils a male need for supremacy and self-righteousness. Another stereotyping that is resented is evident in what Gilbert and Gubar call "linguistic misogyny"[59] which paints woman as a stupid, babbling creature whose words are incoherent, sheer nonsense, and destructive. It explores language as a vehicle of distorting woman's position as a human being.

Helene Cixous by deconstructing the fairy tale of the "sleeping beauty" shows how passivity in woman has been seen desirable. A beauty who is sleeping, not living but only existing, is acceptable. Beautiful dolls dancing to the tunes of their husbands are welcome, but living, thinking individuals are not:

> She sleeps, she is intact, eternal, absolutely powerless. He has no doubt that she has been waiting for him forever. The secret of her beauty, kept for him: she has the perfection of something finished. Or not begun. However, she is breathing. Just enough life – and not too much. Then he will kiss her. So that when she opens her eyes she will see only *him*; him in place of everything, all-him.... She is lying down, he stands up. She arises – end of the dream – what follows is socio-cultural: he makes her lots of babies, she spends her youth in labour; from bed to bed, until the age at which the thing isn't "woman" for him anymore.[60]

Feminist criticism attempts to revise the traditional "patriarchal" canon by bringing to consciousness and into print a number of previously neglected books. It exposes sexist bias in the mainstream "canons" which deliberately marginalized works of women writers.

Feminist criticism also exposes and rejects sexist criticism. Male critics often assess a woman's writing on the premise that any book written by a woman is necessarily inferior and flawed. Male critics often cite personal life of the woman writers to interpret their fiction. Such sexist bias in male critics is termed as "Phallic Criticism" by Mary Ellman. She says:

> Like eruptions from physical desire, this intellectual distraction is no less frequent being gratuitous as well. . . . Books by women authors are treated as if they were women themselves, and criticism embarks, at its happiest, upon an intellectual measuring of hips and busts.[61]

Such sexist bias in literature and criticism is decried by feminist critics as it is not guided by reason or logic. They, in fact, insist that literary evaluation should be asexual.

Emphasizing the political nature of feminist criticism, Toril Moi defines feminist criticism as follows:

> "Feminist criticism" . . . is a specific kind of political discourse: a critical and theoretical practice committed to the struggle against patriarchy and sexism, not simply a concern for gender in literature, at least not if the latter is presented as no more than another interesting critical approach on a line with a concern for sea-imagery or metaphors of war in medieval poetry. . . . There are, of course, different political views within the feminist camp. My point here is . . . simply to insist that recognizable feminist criticism and theory must in some way be relevant to the study of the social, institutional and personal power relations between the sexes.[62]

She also distinguishes between the often confused terms "feminist," "feminine" and "femaleness." "Feminism" is described as "a political situation," "femaleness" as a matter of biology and "femininity" as a set of culturally defined characteristics.[63] Toril Moi insists on the necessity of deconstructing the opposition between the traditionally "masculine" and "feminine" values and to confront the full political force and reality of such categories. The very fact of being female does not necessarily guarantee a feminist approach. Works by women on women writers also do not necessarily exemplify anti-patriarchal commitment. A feminist critic has political commitment to fight against all forms of exploitation of women.

While feminist criticism has a definite ideology, it does not have a methodology. It is interdisciplinary in nature and uses material from such diverse disciplines as linguistics, psychology, anthropology, sociology, history, etc. Hence a feminist critic's approach is pluralistic, drawing on various schools of thought such as Marxism, psycho-analysis, structuralism, existentialism and deconstruction.

Despite extensive and significant work being done by feminist critics, certain questions remain still unanswered – whether there is a distinctively female or patriarchal style, or mode of consciousness, or type of literature; its relations to the androgynous reality of persons, etc. Though there is often a mention of a different kind of aesthetics in feminist works yet there is so far no clear definition of a "feminist aesthetic."

Some limitations apart, feminist criticism has been a major critical revolution. It has helped in infusing necessary courage in women writers to write about their own emotions and experience, boldly and unselfconsciously, which were earlier considered as personal and trivial. It has also provided a fresh perspective to study literature by demythologizing the claim that the male perspective is the universal human perspective. It has also helped in destroying the primacy of "the Anglo-American (White, male, middle-class) canon by adding to 'literature' both specifically female and popular elements."[64] It has also done a major job in raising consciousness in gender-related issues, thus promoting the goals of feminist movement and hoping for some gradual change in the stereotype division of gender roles.

NOTES

1. Ephesians 5: 22.
2. In *The Holy Bible*, there is another reference to this effect: "This is now bone of my bones and flesh of my flesh: She shall be called woman, because she was taken out of man." (Genesis 2: 13).
3. Shaikh M. H. Kidwai, *Woman* (Delhi: Seema, 1976), p. 20.
4. *Ibid.*
5. Marilyn French, *Shakespeare's Division of Experience* (1982; rpt. London: Abacus, 1983), p. 15.
6. Quoted in Mary Wollstonecraft, *A Vindication of the Rights of Woman* (1972), ed. Miriam Brody Kramnick (Harmondsworth: Penguin, 1975), p. 179.
7. Quoted in Kate Millett, *Sexual Politics* (1969; rpt, London: Rupert Hart-Davis, 1971), p. 74.
8. *Manusmriti*, III, 56, in *Manav Dharma Shastra,* trans. and ed. Graves Chamnen Haughton, vol. III (New Delhi: Cosmo, 1982), p. 68.
9. *Great Women of India*, ed. Swami Madhavananda and Ramesh Chandra Majumdar (Mayavati, Almora: Advaita Ashrama, 1953), p. xv. The book includes separate comprehensive articles on the position of Indian women during the different ages from ancient times to modern

times. References to ancient Indian epics noted parenthetically in the text are to this edition.

10. Abinas Chandra Bose, *Hymns from the Vedas* (Bombay: Asia, 1965), p.12.
11. Marilyn French, *Beyond Power: On Women, Men and Morals* (1985; rpt. London: Abacus, 1986), p. xvi.
12. *Ibid.*, p. 23.
13. *The Koran*, trans. J.M. Rodwell (Hertz: Everyman's Library, 1909), p. 415.
14. Kidwai, p. 14.
15. Quoted in Simone de Beauvoir, *The Second Sex*, trans. and ed. H.M. Parshley (1953; rpt. Harmondsworth: Penguin, 1983), p. 22.
16. Quoted in Tara Ali Baig, *India's Woman Power* (New Delhi: S. Chand, 1976), p. 57.
17. Nalinaksha Dutt, "Great Women in Buddhism," *Great Women of India*, p. 254.
18. Kidwai, p. 8.
19. Uma Chakravarti, "The Development of the Sita Myth: A Case Study of Women in Myth and Literature," *Samya Shakti: A Journal of Women's Studies*, I, No. 1 (July 1983), p. 70.
20. Neera Desai and Maithreyi Krishnaraj, *Women and Society in India* (Delhi: Ajanta, 1987), p.29.
21. Kuppuswamy, in *Social Change in India* (1972; rpt. New Delhi: Vikas, 1982), p.241, opines: "it appears as if several drastic social changes took place in the Indian society from about B.C. 300 to the beginning of the Christian era which led to the curtailment of freedom of women."
22. Uma Vasudev, "Women," *Change and Conflict in India*, ed. Romesh Thapar (Madras: Macmillan, 1978), p. 62.
23. *Time*, 7 April 1986, p. 30, reports a sex harassment case of Mechelle Vinson who was forced to have sex with her boss, forty times or so against her wishes. Repeated pleadings by Vinson to leave her alone went unheard and she was threatened with being deprived of her job and her life. The news reporter concludes the report with the comment: "That situation is unlikely to change whether the Supreme Court rules for or against Mechelle Vinson."
24. Mary Wollstonecraft, p. 82.
25. Quoted in Germaine Greer, *The Female Eunuch* (1970; rpt. St. Albana: Paladin, 1976), p. 59.
26. Wollstonecraft, p. 131.

27. Quoted in Millett, p. 68.
28. Quoted in *The Rights and Wrongs of Women*, ed. Juliet Mitchell and Ann Oakley (Harmondsworth: Penguin, 1976), p. 334.
29. William H. Cafe, *Woman and Equality* (New York: Oxford University Press, 1977), p. 24.
30. *Ibid.*, p.16.
31. Quoted in Pratima Asthana, *Women's Movement in India* (Delhi: Vikas, 1974), p. 57.
32. Neera Desai and Maithreyi Krishnaraj in *Women and Society in India* make a thorough study of the role being played by various women organizations in India, in the chapter "Women's Organizations." The Hyderabad-based Progressive Organization of Women, Bombay-based Socialist Women's Group or Forum Against Oppression of Women are some of the womens's groups established during the 1970s in India and have initiated "anti-rape movement." These groups have succeeded in campaigning against rape and in unfolding certain cases where police were involved in sexual molestation of innocent women.
33. Simone de Beauvoir, p. 16.
34. Betty Friedan, *The Feminine Mystique* (1963; rpt. Harmondsworth: Penguin, 1971), p. 9.
35. Kate Millett, p. 23.
36. Germaine Greer, p. 18.
37. Quoted in Juliet Mitchell, *Psychoanalysis and Feminism* (1974; rpt. Harmondsworth: Penguin, 1975), p. 340 (F.N.).
38. Shulamith Firestone, *The Dialectic of Sex* (New York: William Morrow, 1970), p. 16.
39. *Woman in Sexist Society: Studies in Power and Powerlesness*, ed. Vivian Gornick and Barbara K. Moran (New York: New American Library, Mentor Books, 1972).
40. Sheila Rowbotham, *Women, Resistance and Revolution* (New York: Pantheon, 1972), p. 11.
41. Juliet Mitchell and Ann Oakley, p. 11.
42. Isa Kapp, "Women's Liberation in America," *SPAN*, 15, No. 1 (Jan. 1974), p. 27.
43. Angela Weir and Elizabeth Wilson, "The British Women's Movement," *New Left Review*, No. 148, (Nov./Dec. 1984), p. 77. In this essay the writers deal in detail with the socialist feminism as it exists in Britain today.

44. Juliet Mitchell, "Women and Equality," *The Rights and Wrongs of Women*, p. 380.
45. Weir and Wilson, p.77.
46. *Ibid.*, p.79.
47. Toril Moi, "Feminist Literary Criticism," *Modern Literary Theory*, ed. Ann Jefferson and David Robey (1982; rpt. London: B.T. Batsford, 1986), p. 212.
48. *Ibid.*, p. 214.
49. Betty Friedan, *The Second Stage* (New York: Summit, 1981), p. 341.
50. Marilyn French, p. 478.
51. Virginia Woolf, *Contemporary Writers* (London: Hogarth, 1965), p. 26.
52. Suzanne Hall, "Feminist Writing," *Literature Alive*, I, No. 2 (Sept. 1987), p. 4.
53. Marilyn French, p. 518.
54. Sandra M. Gilbert, "A Tarantella of Theory," Introduction to Helene Cixous and Catherine Clement's *The Newly Born Woman* (1975), trans. Betsy Wings (Manchester: Manchester Univesity Press, 1975), p. xvi.
55. Quoted by Sandra M. Gilbert, p. xvi
56. As reported in *The Tribune*, 7 May 1988, p.7, these seven universities are "Kerala, Punjab, Nehru, Ranchi, Banaras, South Gujarat and SNDT Women's University."
57. Cheri Register, "Literary Criticism," *Signs*, 6 (1980), p. 268.
58. Ruth Yeazell, "Fictional Heroines and Feminist Criticism," *Novel*, 8 (Fall 1974), p. 29.
59. Sandra M.Gilbert and Susan Gubar, *No Man's Land: The Place of the Woman Writer in the Twentieth Century* (London: Yale Univeristy Press, 1988), p. 231.
60. Helene Cixous, p. 66.
61. Mary Ellman, *Thinking about Women* (New York: Harcourt Brace Jovanovich, 1968), p. 29.
62. Toril Moi, p. 204.
63. *Loc. cit.*
64. Grant Webster, "American Literary Criticism: A Bibliographical Essay," *American Studies International*, xx, I (Autumn 1981), p. 20.

Woman Made Woman

> One is not born, but rather becomes a woman. No biological, psychological or economic fate determines the figure that the human female presents in society; it is civilization as a whole that produces this creature, intermediate between male and eunuch, which is described as feminine. (Simone De Beauvoir, *The Second Sex*)

In a patriarchal society, a female child is brought up under the strict control of her parents with the view that she is to be given to a new master, her husband, who will determine and shape her for the rest of her life. The traditional feminine virtues and graces are instilled in her so that she could be an attractive commodity in the marriage market. She is groomed to be an object of sale right from her childhood. She gets hardly any encouragement to develop her independent individual self. The decision in terms of her career or even marriage is taken by her father, brother or mother. As Simone De Beauvoir observes, "Marriage is the destiny traditionally offered to women by society."[1] Marriage is considered to be the greatest ambition of a girl. As such a woman is always someone's daughter, someone's wife or someone's mother, minus her own identity. The feminists highly resent these culturally constructed norms which make women subjects of men in various forms. They do not deny the biological differences between a male and a female, but there is no reason to presume, as men do, that these physical differences make them superior to women. The feminists maintain that woman is not born but made by the society.[2]

The patriarchal practices which reduce women's status to inferior social beings are further perpetuated by myths and traditions which unfortunately have been embedded in the fabric of every society. According to V.A. Novarra, the myth related to the role of women in Britain prescribes that "a mother should devote herself to providing a secure environment for her small children. A married woman cannot pursue a career which demands mobility. Works of art by women still have to be judged as "women's work." Membership of an all-male club or society can be prestigious: membership of a woman's organisation is a subject for facetious remarks."[3] In India, since woman is considered to be an "embodiment of sacrifice, silent suffering, humility, faith and knowledge,"[4] she should be virtuous, chaste, submissive, homely, graceful, and devoted to her husband and his family. She must seek pleasure in these relationships. The faintest of any such ideas that every being "exists primarily for the realization of oneself can never occur to her in the wildest of her dreams."[5] These attitudes exemplify the belief that woman should not have any right on her own; that she has only duties in relation to man.

The young women of today are becoming aware of the biased attitude of the society. They have started asserting their individuality by challenging the taboos and destructive social norms. Despite some achievements in educational, professional and legal fields, they have yet to go a long way for their acceptance as equal beings in the prejudiced society where discrimination is practised against women right from birth.

Nayantara Sahgal and Doris Lessing, both place their women characters, mostly with good educational background, in conflict with a parochial society and depict their struggle to pop out of their shells. Though in the novels taken up for study the focus is mainly on the suffering of women within marriage, yet we also get a glimpse of the attempts made to condition her personality along sexist lines before marriage.

In the character of Nita in *This Time of Morning*, Sahgal explores the place of a woman in Indian society before marriage. Nita is the young, beautiful daughter of Dr. Narang, who is a queer blend of Eastern and Western Culture. While Western life style – drinks, dance and bridge – is part of his culture, when it comes to his daughter, he would act in the most traditional manner, imposing severe restrictions on the movement of his ambitious daughter. The Narangs never send their daughter unescorted to parties; as Mrs. Narang puts it: "We don't allow Nita to go out alone. Her father would not hear of it."[6] The Narangs's concern for the safety and protection of their daughter exemplifies their conformity to traditional values. Sahgal refers to the rigid social codes in her *A Time to be Happy*, where Sanad, a young officer working in a foreign company "Selkirk and Lowe," wants to spend his evening with girls like his English officers but dare not do it, because "well brought up young Indian women did not go out with young men unchaperoned. To be seen alone in public with a man would have been a scandal enough for the rigid code of a provincial town."[7]

In her essay "Women: Persons or Possessions," Nayantara Sahgal condemns such attitudes which value women as "property and discourage individuality in them:

> When I heard someone remark "we never allow our daughter to go out" or "I can't do that, my husband would not like it," it sounded a very peculiar, alien jargon. As if, I thought, women were property, not persons.[8]

In a traditional society when a young girl reaches puberty, her movements are restricted, whereas there are no restrictions for her brothers at that age. The double standards start operating more overtly from this stage, binding girls indoors and encouraging boys to develop outdoor activities. A spirit of competition, exploration and challenge is inculcated among boys, and they are taught to assert their supremacy over the world in general. Girls, on the contrary, are discouraged from showing aggressive modes of behaviour and, instead, feminine virtues of grace, modesty and self-effacement are frequently demanded from them.

Nita's parents would not allow their daughter to smoke, to have drinks or attend club dances till she is married. When Rakesh as an escort takes her to a ball one evening, *en route* she questions these conventions:

> "I really would like a cigarette," said Nita.
> "You can't have one."
> "Well, I keep cigarettes in my room. Daddy doesn't know. Isn't it silly not being allowed to do anything until one is married?" (32)

Marriage seems to be a licence to do things hitherto prohibited. Mrs. Narang who speaks fluent English, and "had been a beauty" (148) once, has friends who would gather around the card table and discuss marriage plans of their daughters. There is a "parade of coffee-drinking, canasta-playing women who streamed through the house" (148) of Narangs. Nita abhors this "Victorian culture" and only pines for "a little latitude, some breathing space." (148) In her book *The Feminine Mystique*, Betty Friedan has suggested that a woman can find fulfilment only in some creative work of her own. Nita too has a thirst to do something, and does not want to be bound by nuptial knots as yet. She requests Rakesh to influence her parents in the matter: "I don't want to marry at all just yet. Now you're back, Rakesh, do persuade Mummy and Daddy I should have a job. It's ghastly doing nothing." (32) Later her parents do allow her to take up a job but for a very different reason. Kalyan, a Minister, had offered the job and they simply "didn't have the heart to refuse" (147) a Minister's offer. But Nita looks for something more than merely a job; she strives for independence and her individual identity. She thinks: "a job was never enough. . . . A job led to money and freedom, and freedom demanded a flat of one's own, away from the prying eyes and inquisitive voices" (148) of men and women who do not permit women to gratify their basic needs of self-fulfilment. Betty Friedan accuses society of considering "identity crisis" as man's problem only. The crises of growing up, of choosing his identity, the decision as to what one is and is going to be,"[9] are considered only male prerogatives, and women are told that "truly feminine women do not want careers, higher education, political rights, the independence and the opportunities."[10] Conforming to these tenets, in Indian society the efforts of most of the parents are to find a suitable match of their choice for their daughters. Nita's parents also want to settle down their daughter in marriage and wash their hands of her. They do not give any importance to the wishes of their daughter and force her to marry the man of their choice whom she neither loves nor admires. Nita's suitor is an eligible bachelor, rich and pleasant-mannered and "she had nothing against him, only she did not want to marry him" (149) because she cannot reconcile herself to the fact that Vijay is a stranger "with whom she would spend her life, whose name and children she would bear." (150) However, she fails to assert herself in refusing to marry a man of her parents's choice. And Mrs. Narang is certainly a woman who subscribes to the conventions where women not only "accept stereotype images but also pass them on to their children."[11] She also proves to be an oppressive force when she compels her daughter to marry "one of those men they introduced her to at parties." (148)

At a party in Rakesh's house, Nita dances with her fiancee Vijay. Rakesh, glancing at the pair, says to Saira, "She does not look very happy," (167) to which she replies sarcastically: " 'She says she doesn't know him very well.' The American girl from U.S.I.S looked at them puzzled. 'She doesn't? Why's she marrying him?' 'She'll know him better after they're married,' said Saira." (167-68)

Nita feels utterly unhappy and a sense of uneasiness overpowers her when she learns about her parents's decision to marry her off to a stranger. But the desire to be her own self leads her to commit a *faux pas*, when she gets involved with an elderly man, Kalyan. When she first meets him, she "stood mesmerized in front of him." (135) She finds a strange comfort in his company and visits him frequently on the pretext of decorating his drawing room. Once she refuses to go home and frankly expresses her love for Kalyan:

> "But don't make me go."
> He rose from his chair, "Nita . . ."
> She got up, too, and came like a sleep walker into his arms, clinging to

him.

"Don't make me go, please don't make me go." He took her by the hand and then to his room. (152)

Nita's pre-marital involvement is not the result of the Western liberated life-style: it is an attempt to fulfil her inner desire for love and communication. As Jasbir Jain opines about Nita's sexual involvement with Kalyan, "with Kalyan Sinha, sex comes naturally to her not because he loves her but because she has unconsciously allowed herself to love and admire him and turn to him in her desperation at being hedged in by convention."[12] Though Nita is engaged, emotionally she is still dependant on Kalyan and often meets him to shower her tenderness on him. She tells him: "You gave me the freedom to be myself. I had never had that before. I'd never have known it but for you," (219) and she finally admits: "I've been so happy with you." (220) Nita in fact is the "product of the dichotomies in her upbringing."[13] On the one hand she is brought up in accordance with the liberated life-style, but when the time comes to decide about her marriage, her parents decide her future and she is supposed to silently submit to her wishes.

Through the character of Nita, Sahgal seems to be exposing conventional narrow-minded Indian society, where life-partners are chosen by the parents: the parents arrange for the two young souls to live happily ever after. Sahgal strongly attacks this social convention and names this kind of marriage "just organised rape."[14] Though here she sounds like *avant garde* feminists who reject the institution of marriage and motherhood, yet she does not reject either of the two but advocates harmonious relationships and individual liberties in her novels. She also condemns the hypocrisies of the affluent upper-classes where women are encouraged to take drinks or to smoke in the name of the freedom and modernity (which, however, is a taboo for women belonging to the middle or lower classes in Indian society), but are not allowed to take independent decision in choosing their life partners.

Doris Lessing in *Martha Quest* (Book I of *Children of Violence*) focuses on this aspect of women's problem and shows that a woman has no choice but to bow down to social conventions, traditions and moral obligations. In *Martha Quest*, Lessing traces various stages in the personality of Martha who passes from girlhood to womanhood on a farm in Rhodesia. Mrs. Quest is shaping Martha strictly according to English traditions and putting many "don'ts" in her dress and make-up. She does not like that Martha should meet men, especially Jewish shopkeepers – the Cohen boys – for several reasons. But as far as Martha is concerned, "talking to them exhilarated her, everything seemed easy. She walked over to the Kaffir store when her parents made the trip to the station; sometimes she got a lift from a passing car. Sometimes, though secretly, since this was forbidden, she rode on her bicycle. But there was always an uneasiness about this friendship, because of Mrs. Quest; only last week she had challenged Martha. Being what she was, she could not say outright. "I don't want you to know Jewish shopkeepers."[15] Martha not only defies her mother's wish of remaining aloof from the Cohen boys, but on the contrary becomes more friendly with them and frankly tells her mother one day:

> "I want to see the Cohen boys."
> "You're making friends with them?" demurred Mrs. Quest.
> "I thought we always were friends with them," said Martha scornfully. (46)

Martha is very articulate in pronouncing her choices. As compared to Nita who does not have the courage to tell her parents about her aspirations, Martha expresses her likes and dislikes boldly, openly and in a more defiant manner. Mrs. Quest wants that her daughter should not go alone on the streets as she is afraid of the black natives who often rape white girls. But here also Martha opposes her mother and announces: "If I don't get a lift, I'll walk," which in itself was a daring step as it "infringed one of the taboos—'young white girl walking alone,' etc." (46) Martha Quest, in fact is an idealist in revolt against the snobbery of her parents. She tries to live life to the full with every nerve, emotion and instinct bared to experience.

In a patriarchal society, the birth of a female child is traditionally less welcome than that of the male. Being born a boy is itself a privilege. Investment in the upbringing of a girl is relatively less: the major goal for her being marriage, she is looked down upon as a transitory member of the family in contrast with the boy, who is supposed to be the transmitter of the family name to future generations and is, therefore, more carefully and lovingly brought up and given more advantages. This is true not only of Indian society, but also of the white society in British colonies like Rhodesia where similar attitudes prevail. Martha Quest also becomes aware of how gender discrimination is practised in her family. While her younger brother with "half her brains" was put in an "expensive school, like a visitor from a more prosperous world," (34) she was studying in a local school. The awareness of the biased attitude makes her self-reliant and defiant towards her parents and she decides to seek her own identity outside the parental hold.

Mrs. Quest, in her youth, had been a "pretty and athletic-looking English girl with light-brown hair and blue eyes as candid as spring sunshine, and she was now exactly as she would have been had she remained in England." (10) Now in Rhodesia, she is looking after her farmer husband and teenage daughter with utmost care, like a typical English matron. Like Mrs. Narang, she also warns Martha against "walking alone" (46) on the streets and imposes several limitations on her wearing lipstick or latest dresses. She considers women who use cosmetics "as fast." (13) She wants her daughter to be a different girl from the bunch of fast girls and "did not consider her daughter to be on a level with Marnie, whom she found in altogether bad taste, wearing grown up clothes and lipstick at fifteen and talking about boys." (13) Mrs. Quest, like all mothers, wants her daughter to maintain her dignity as she thinks, "a man will never marry a girl he does not respect." (12) In the West too, traditional women bring up their daughters keeping in view the likes and dislikes of men.

Despite several restrictions, Maratha finally rebels against her parents. One day standing before the mirror, she took a pair of scissors and severed the bodice from the shirt of her dress. She was trying to make the folds like Marnie's when the door suddenly opened, and her father came in. Looking at Martha, he remarked: "Your mother won't like you cutting her dresses to pieces." She said defiantly: "Daddy, why should I wear dresses like a kid of ten?" And when her mother enters the scene, she argues:

> "I'm sixteen," said Martha, between set teeth, in a stifled voice,...
> "My dear, nice girls don't wear clothes like this until..."
> "I'm not a nice girl," broke in Martha, and suddenly burst into laughter. (21)

Since financial independence is necessary to seek security and liberation, Martha puts in all her efforts to take up some job without letting her parents know about her plans. Finally she gets a job in the town, with the help of her Jewish friend Joss Cohen, but unlike Nita who asks Rakesh to persuade her parents in the matter, Martha informs her parents about her achievement only after getting it. When Joss writes her about the vacancy in his uncle's firm, "she felt as if a phase of her life has ended, and that now a new one should begin; . . . With Joss's letter in her hand, she walked onto the veranda, and informed her parents, in a hasty way, that she was taking a job in town; and she hardly heard their startled queries. It all seemed so easy now. 'But you can't expect me to stay here for the rest of my life'!" (90-91) As is expected of a girl like Martha, bold and defiant, she unlike Nita decides to marry a man of her own choice: she chooses a civil servant and informs her parents about the marriage ten days before the ceremony.

The two novels reveal that a traditional mother whether in England or in India wants her daughter to be a "good" girl and "properly married." Simone de Beauvoir says that "a generous mother who sincerely seeks her child's welfare, will as a rule think that it is wiser to make a 'true woman' of her, since society will more readily accept her if this is done."[16] Mrs. Quest and Mrs. Narang try to fulfil their duties as mothers by bringing up their daughters as models of grace, although both Nita and Martha resent the maternal authority. Times have changed since their mothers's days and moreover they are socially aware girls rather than conforming girls who happily accept their roles.

While portraying mother-daughter relationship, Lessing depicts conflict in it most of the time. In *Martha Quest*, Mrs. Quest tries to project herself upon Martha and tries to model her daughter according to her own wishes. Martha revolts against her and asserts her independence but Mrs. Quest feels betrayed. Both Mrs. Narang and Mrs. Quest act as alert guardians of their daughters. Desirous of their welfare, they do not want that society should raise a finger at them. They want to bring them up as graceful, dignified young girls, who would be in high demand in the marriage market. Discussing the mother-daughter relationship, Simone de Beauvoir observes: "the daughter is for the mother at once her double and another person, the mother is at once overweeningly affectionate and hostile towards her daughter: she saddles her child with her own destiny: a way of revenging herself for it."[17] In other words, a daughter is an alter ego of her mother. The mother wants to realize her unfulfilled dreams through her daughter.

Lessing's *The Grass is Singing*, however, depicts a very different mother-daughter relationship. Mary often shares her mother's sorrows, who has been a victim of male-oppression. She would often comfort her mother who is unhappy and weeps silently or sometimes openly resents her drunkard husband. Her mother "made a confidante of Mary early. . . . Mary comforted her miserable longing to get away, but feeling important too, and hating her father."[18] And after the death of her mother whenever Mary is reminded of her, she remembers her in terms of miseries. Till the age of thirty, Mary does not marry as the unhappy memories of her childhood and miseries of her mother flash before her eyes, every time she thinks of marriage, though finally she too is entrapped in this institution by the society.

If an Indian girl brought up under strict parental control suddenly gets freedom, the results could again be disastrous because of her ignorance or over-protective upbringing that does not allow her to see things for herself. Nita in *This Time of Morning* is striving for independence and dying to "get abroad" (30) whereas in this novel itself, there is another character, Leela, who succeeds in going to America but gets a "cultural shock" in the alien society and finally commits suicide in desperation. Leela, who belongs to a "modest, unpretentious" (77) Hindu family of Banaras, is studying in Redcliffe. In America, she gets every freedom which a young girl like Nita cherishes: lipstick, dancing, smoking and going out with young men. She has taken this at first "with the tremulous flutter of a bird just uncaged, and later with a soaring delight in every aspect of her new freedom." (58) She gets her lovely long hair cut off in short swinging bob, yet in this new environment she moves uncertainly as if "shrinking from some of the inevitable outcomes of freedom." (58) But then "she had been a girl and a sheltered one and Banaras was no preparation for America." (77) Soon she realizes that she is pregnant and drowns herself in a river. Her pregnancy had been an "emotional shock" (76) for her and out of shame and desperation she takes this fatal decision. Leela could have come out of the difficult situation through medical help and lived normally as before. She, however, does not think of ways of escape, because her culture and society did not train her for this kind of situation. In India, normally, young girls are not supposed to know or talk about sex before marriage. Leela fails to strike a balance between the old values and the new-found freedom. Hence, she pays for it. Sahgal is concerned with the question of how far different conventions and traditions imply a fundamental difference in moral outlook: how far an Indian girl could accept Western conventions and form Western tastes without losing her integrity and independence.

While there may be no harm in knowing about sex before marriage, to be involved in such an act before marriage for a woman is concerned to be the highest sin in Indian society. Sahgal conveys this in *Storm in Chandigarh* through Saroj who is leading a miserable life with her husband, Inder. Bitterness comes in their life when Inder comes to know of Saroj's past. Sahgal does not focus much on Saroj's life before marriage: we know only that Saroj during her college days was friendly with one of the college mates, who would visit her house quite often. Out of curiosity she once had sex with him. But later when Inder comes to know of it, he treats her brutally and considers her a sinner. He would punish her quite often and torture her physically and mentally:

> When Inder could not sleep he resurrected the other man, the one who had known Saroj before he had, making her marriage a mockery and betrayal. He had stalked the man down the dark alleys of his imagination, his thought about him churning, now sticking, now moving sluggishly, now flowing on unimpeded like the filth in the city's sewers. *If I catch him I shall kill him.*[19]

Ironically, Inder is torturing his wife for having pre-marital relationship once only, that too in innocence, while he had no explanation to offer for his own extra-marital relationship with another man's wife. These double standards make one of Sahgal's characters comment angrily:

> It always amazes me what is taken for granted in a man is horrifying in a woman. Even in this day and age. Imagine.[20]

In Indian society, the one unpardonable crime for an unmarried girl is to have a sexual intercourse with any man, though, strangely enough, it is considered no crime at all for a man to have sexual relations with other girls before or after his marriage.

Young women in Sahgal's fictional world are the helpless victims of the taboo-ridden, conventional society. Instead of asserting themselves or fighting against the odds, some of them easily accept the role traditionally offered to them, while some others opt for death as the ultimate solution to the mundane man-made problems. Madhu in *A Situation in New Delhi* after being raped by a group of university students in the Registrar's office, finds no sympathy from her parents or from the society, and ultimately chooses to burn herself to death. When she is hospitalized after the rape, she is crying in agony but the nurse puts her hand on her mouth to stop her, the gestures becomes symbolic of the authoritarian forces trying to stop the cries of innocent sufferers. Further, it appears that the nurse, a woman, is conveying to the victims the need to suffer in silence, for cries can cause curiosity and thus lead to a scandal. The nurse might be a wise and experienced woman who knows women are to suffer in silence and cries will make the matters only worse for the victim. Like Leela in *This Time of Morning*, she finds no one who would help her in distress. She needed care, love and sympathy of her parents, instead she finds herself isolated and a burden on her parents, who in turn want to get rid of her by marrying her off and consult many astrologers about it. The astrologers too assure them that she would be married within a year or so. Madhu, however, does not want to marry and even seeks a prominent lady minister Devi's help in the matter. Madhu's parents do not want that the neighbours should know about the incident of rape as this may lead to their social ostracization: "She screamed in the night and at home they said she was going mad the way she carried on." (61) At home, no one pays attention to her emotional needs or shares her grief. Four days after her return from the hospital, she resumes her studies in the university and her brother is made incharge of her till "they could hand her to another household." (61) But before they can settle her marriage with a man from Delhi, she decides her fate otherwise. Even if she had been married, once the incident was known, she would have been condemned to perpetual misery. How can the society pardon her for her loss of virginity, when it did not forgive Saroj for the same reason! Perceiving the consequences, Madhu took the fatal decision of burning herself to death, instead of leading a miserable life even after marriage.

Through this incident of rape, Sahgal's purpose is not merely to depict the hooliganism and disorder in the educational institutions, but to show that a woman in a patriarchal set up has no place to go to once she is stigmatized. This incident is just an example of the reality of women's position in the society. "Clearly Sahgal has very strong feelings about the wastage of young lives, especially women's lives."[21]

In our social set-up, the parents of a girl do not act boldly and firmly out of fear of the society. Instead of bringing the guilty ones to law for punishment, they prefer to suppress the matter because they know all too well the hypocrisics of the society. Conforming to the social ways, they keep their daughters secure in the four walls of their house till they are handed over to their rightful masters.

In a traditional society, those women can be happy who blindly and unthinkingly accept the roles it assigns them. Pinky, a happy girl, is very enthusiastic about her marriage and obediently consents to her parents's choice: "Girls like Pinky lived as their mother and grandmother had." (42) She does not know anything about sex or contraceptives. Her mother thinks, "It's rubbish, this modern business about knowing everything before you marry." (41) She probably forgets that due to the lack of sex-education, Pinky would be soon drifting into motherhood as she is drifting into marriage. Pinky is the unthinking type of character who has no regrets and willingly accepts the traditional role.

Pinky is very much conscious of her looks and figure and visits "Beauty Parlours" to "get her arms and legs done, leaving her skin with a polished look, not a hair in sight." (147) At home also she finds no other pastime than to care for her elbows and eyebrows. Pinky's desire to look beautiful represents her submission to the patriarchal values according to which women are "to be mere dolls for men."[22] Men mostly prefer doll-like beautiful girls as their wives who should always give them pleasure and never question any of their ideas or actions. Girls like Pinky help in perpetuating patriarchal set-up. But Sahgal does not approve of this type of women. Pinky remains a minor character. The central character in Sahgal's novels is a thinking wcman striving for an individual, independent personality.

Pinky's friends Tazi and Reba are equally immature and very enthusiastic about the idea of marriage. Their conception of marriage is that one can live one's "own life, away from prying supervision." (148) Ironically, these girls believe that "marriage was a change. At least you got out from under your parents." (148) For them marriage is an escape from the control of parents. These immature girls see marriage in terms of gaudy clothes, outings and lots of fun. They have no idea that marriage means only changing masters – first parents were there, now there will be husband. As Simone de Beauvoir observes: "There is a unanimous agreement that getting a husband – or in some cases a 'protector' – is for her the most important of undertakings. . . . She will free herself from the parental home, from her mother's hold, she will open up her future not by active conquest but by delivering herself up, passive and docile, into the hands of a new master."[23] Girls like Pinky, Tazi and Reba cherish a rosy picture of marriage and are not at all aware of the obligations involved in this relationship. These purely "feminine women," to use a phrase from Sheila Rowbotham, are unlike other intelligent and sensitive women of Sahgal. Discussing "feminine women," Sheila Rowbotham observes: "The 'feminine' woman in making herself prey tries to reduce man, also, to her carnal passivity: she occupies herself in catching him in her trap, in enchaining him by means of the desire she arouses in him in submissively making herself a thing."[24] Pinky and other girls are as carefree as birds and are unaware of the other side of the life, which is full of complex problems – problems of understanding, adjustments etc. in marriage. Society, however, considers such girls an excellent species for making wives and these girls find a comfortable place in it.

Not only in the East, in the West too marriage is considered to be the final destiny for women. Mary, in Lessing's *The Grass is Singing*, is almost forced into marriage by society. Mary, who is different from Pinky, Nita or Martha, does not experience much parental restriction, but gets shattered at a remark from a friend. Mary had an unhappy and disturbing childhood because of her drunkard father who would constantly torture her mother. She spent the most part of her girlhood in a boarding school, free from any subservience. At sixteen, she took a job in some office in the town and was very happy with her "comfortable carefree existence."[25] At twenty, she first lost her mother and subsequently lost her father too. This removed the "last link that bound her to a childhood she hated to remember." (37) She was happily spending her spare time in games or in the cinema houses and never thought of courtship or marriage. She dreaded marriage because when "she thought of marriage she remembered her father coming home red-eyed and fuddled; when she thought of children she saw her mother's face at her children's funerals – anguished, but as dry and as hard as rock. Mary liked other people's children but shuddered at the thought of having any of her own." (40) As Lorna Sage says, although Mary is "emotionally blocked by her parents's poverty and misery and her mother's contempt for her father,"[26] yet she is not unhappy. But then a turning point comes in her life when she overhears her intimate friends discussing her age and marriage. She is horrified to hear them commenting that there is "something missing somewhere" (42) in her, just because she, not thirty, is still unmarried. This little incident leaves a profound impact on Mary. "She was thrown completely off her balance because some gossiping women had said she ought to get married." (46) The tension in her life as a single woman begins here, and she is made to search frantically for a husband, despite her ardent dislike for marriage. She comes across a widower of fifty-five with half-grown children. His proposal is unthinkingly accepted by Mary, but once when that man tries to kiss her, she comes out from the house into the night and weeps bitterly. This incident becomes the talk of the town. At that crisis, she comes across Dick Turner an ambitious farmer whom she meets casually at the cinema and decides to marry, despite their different backgrounds, tastes and ambitions. The only common point between the two is that both of them are eager to marry. The marriage, however, turns out to be a failure. Once Mary runs out from his home and thinks of resuming her life as a single woman, but in her old office she is not taken back because now she has lost the graces and attractiveness which are a professional requirement. Roberta Rubenstein rightly observes that *The Grass is Singing* "concerns with social, economic and political structures, with being female in a conventional man's world."[27] Dick follows Mary and takes her back to his home. However, Mary fails to return to her independent and tension-free past which she had enjoyed before marriage.

Both Lessing and Sahgal have portrayed mothers as authority figures stifling the daughters in the name of conforming to traditional values. In Sahgal's *This Time of Morning*, Rashmi's mother Mira is a patriotic leader's devoted wife and expects the same from her daughter. When Rashmi announces her failure in marriage, Mira gets shocked and says: "What reasons under heaven could sever the marriage bond? Women stayed married, had since time immemorial stayed married, under every conceivable circumstance, to brutal insensitive husbands, to lunatics and lepers.... If there was suffering, too, it was a part of life." (146) Mira is a typical Indian woman who "knows of no acceptable alternative role for herself than that of wife-mother," and for her the "mark of her success as a person is in her living, thriving children."[28] Ironically, it is only Rashmi's father who understands her agony and protects her. He supports his daughter to lead a life of her own – a life of self-fulfilment and self-sufficiency. Sahgal in her novels mainly dwells on the problems of women of the educated upper class; hence issues like harassment of poor girls by the in-laws for bringing less dowry or the anxiety of parents about the marriage of their daughters etc. do not receive Sahgal's attention.

Lessing's women Martha and Mary also belong to the privileged "white class" in South Rhodesia, but among the "whites" they are not rich and face the problems of livelihood. Being young unmarried women, they face problems of which Lessing has a first-hand knowledge as Lessing herself has spent the earlier part of her life as a working woman in Rhodesia, prior to settling down in England.

Both Sahgal and Lessing reveal in their novels how before marriage women are brought up strictly according to the traditional codes. The moment a girl reaches adolescence, she is reminded of her femininity. The double standards and dichotomous attitude which continue to operate throughout a woman's life start right in her parents's home. She is prevented from developing her individuality. She is constantly reminded by her mother that a girl is destined for man and the one who gets the most masculine attention is the luckiest one. A woman in a male-dominated society is thus conditioned into the emotional and cognitive traits of subordination and dependence.[29]

Both Sahgal and Lessing insist that a woman needs to throw off much of this conditioning, and learn assertiveness, self-confidence, etc. While some traditional-minded girls accept marriage in order to be free from the parental hold, though under the mistaken notion that marriage will give them freedom, others like Nita and Martha, who do not accept so quietly the commands of the parents, look for individual satisfaction and self-realization. While sometimes the revolt may be partial as in the case of Nita, at other times it may be complete as in the case of Martha who chooses her job and her life partner herself.

Marriage which is considered by some as freedom from parental bondage and by others as way to self-realization, unfortunately turns out to be a sad experience for many women of Sahgal and Lessing as is revealed in the analysis of their position within marriage in the following chapter.

NOTES

1. Simone De Beauvoir, *The Second Sex*, p. 445.
2. The epigraph of *Woman in Sexist Society: Studies in Power and Powerlessness*, "The fault lies not in our stars, our harmones, our menstural cycles or our empty internal spaces, but in our institutions. Woman is made not born."
3. V.A. Novarra, "International Women's Year 1975," *Contemporary Review*, 226, No. 1313 (June 1975), p. 317.
4. Quoted in Jana Matson Everett, *Women and Social Change in India* (New Delhi: Heritage, 1981), p. 76. The complete sentence of Mahatma Gandhi in *Young India*, 15 Sept. 1921, is as follows: "To me the female sex is not the weaker sex. It is the nobler of the two; for it is even today the embodiment of sacrifice, silent suffering humility, faith and knowledge."
5. Akhileshwar Jha, *Modernization and the Hindu Socio-Culture* (Delhi: B.R. Publishing Corporation, 1978), p. 95.
6. Nayantara Sahgal, *This Time of Morning* (1965; rpt. Delhi: Orient Paperbacks, 1970), p. 30.
7. Nayantara Sahgal, *A Time to be Happy* (1957; rpt. New Delhi: Sterling, 1975), p. 116.
8. Nayantara Sahgal, "Women: Persons or Possessions," *Hindustan Times* (Sunday Magazine), 19 July 1970, p. IV: I.
9. Betty Friedan, *The Feminine Mystique*, p. 68.
10. *Ibid.*, p. 13.
11. Ivy Khan, "Tradition vs. Modernity," *Span*, 16, No. 10 (Oct. 1975), p. 20.
12. Jasbir Jain, "The Aesthetics of Morality: Sexual Relations in the Novels of Nayantara Sahgal," *The Journal of Indian Writing in English*, 6, No. 1 (Jan. 1978), p. 42.
13. Feroza Jussawalla, "Of Cabbages and Kings: *This Time of Morning* and *Storm in Chandigarh* by Nayantara Sahgal," *The Journal of Indian Writing in English*, 5, No.1 (Jan. 1977), p. 49.

14. Nayantara Sahgal, *A Situation in New Delhi* (London: Magazine Editions, 1977), p. 25.
15. Doris Lessing, *Martha Quest* (Book I of *Children of Violence* sequence) (1964; rpt. London: Panther, 1984), p. 16.
16. De Beauvoir, p. 309.
17. *Loc. cit.*
18. Doris Lessing, *The Grass is Singing* (1950; rpt. London: Granada, 1980), p. 34.
19. Nayantara Sahgal, *Storm in Chandigarh* (1969; rpt. Delhi Hind Pocket Books, 1970), p. 93.
20. Sahgal, *This Time of Morning*, p. 162.
21. Marcia P. Liu, "Continuity and Development in the Novels of Nayantara Sahgal," *The Journal of Indian Writing in English*, 8, Nos.1-2 (Jan-July 1980), p. 51.
22. G. Alison Raymond, *Half the World's People* (New York: Appleton-Century Crofts, 1965), p. 25.
23. De Beauvoir, p. 352.
24. Sheila Rowbotham, p. 718.
25. Lessing, *The Grass is Singing*, p. 36.
26. Lorna Sage, *Doris Lessing* (London: Methuen, 1982), p. 25.
27. Roberta Rubenstein, *The Novelistic Vision of Doris Lessing: Breaking the Forms of Consciousness* (London: University of Illinois Press, 1979), p. 17.
28. Alfred D'Souza, ed., *Women in Contemporary India* (New Delhi: Manohar, 1977), p. X.
29. The conditioning of woman recommended in a popular feminist ballad is in fact rejected by feminists:

    Well I tried to be the kind of woman you wanted me to be . . .
    Made to please, and not to tease, it's the custom-made woman blues . . .
    And I tried to see life your way, and say all the things you wanted me to say.
    Loving thoughts, gentle hands,
    all guaranteed to keep a hold of your man,
    Made to please, and not to tease,
    it's the custom-made woman blues.

    Quoted in Lynne Segal, *Is the Future Female? Troubled Thoughts on Contemporary Feminism*, p. 118.

Woman as Wife

Helmer: Before everything else, you're a wife and a mother.
Nora: I believe that before everything else I'm a human being—just as much as your are . . . or at any rate I shall try to become one.

Ibsen, *A Doll's House*

Marriage is the deepest as well as the most problematic of all human relations. Sociologists define it as a "cultural phenomenon which sanctions a more or less permanent union between partners conferring legitimacy on their offspring."[1] Religiously marriage is supposed to be the holy union of two souls and bodies. Amongst Hindus, the wife is known as *Ardhangini* or *Sahadharmini,* terms which emphasize her equality and oneness with the husband. In Christianity, the first parents were made "bone of one bone and flesh of one flesh." In marriage, oneness, companionship and mutuality are stressed, and it is assumed that the interests of the husband and wife are one, that whatever is for the benefit of the one is for the benefit of the other also.

Despite these idealized concepts of marriage, woman in reality is essentially a subservient partner in marriage. Marriage often does not mean companionship or equality for her; rather it is a trap which negates her rights to individuality, independence and self-realization. She is subjugated, marginalized and sidelined and usually her position is no better than the poor, oppressed and racial minorities like the blacks. The "power politics," to use a phrase from Kate Millett, operates in a subtle manner in the institution of marriage, reducing the status of a woman to merely a "utility item," an object for decoration, for possession and for man's sexual gratification. Marriage turns out to be an institution of oppression for her in various forms rather than of her protection for which it was primarily insituted.

The feminists differ on the issue whether marriage as an institution should be retained or scrapped totally. Militants like Simone de Beauvoir and Germaine Greer reject it saying that it has been instituted merely to "legalize reproduction" and that it "diminishes man . . . but almost always annihilates woman."[2] Germaine Greer suggests that "if independence is a necessary concomitant of freedom, woman must not marry."[3] Less militant radicals like Betty Friedan suggest alternate ways to make the most of this institution. Friedan insists on pursuing a meaningful activity within marriage itself in order to lead a happy and satisfying married life. Family, she thinks, is a source of women's power and advises women to re-embrace the institution which is "basic to life."[4] Marilyn French emphasizes resurgence and revalorization of feminine values of nurturing and sharing which she feels can save the world from destruction and totalitarianism. Like French, another feminist of the eighties Lynne Segal insists on combining autonomy and alliance in marriage. She finds the "polarised thinking about women and men"[5] quite inadequate in the present context. Women, she believes, have greater humanity and hence can save the world from impending social, ecological and nuclear disasters.

Sahgal and Lessing delineate with keen perception and sensitivity the problems and sufferings of women in marriage, who feel entrapped, oppressed and doomed to the care of husband and home, and show their reaction to it in their novels. Some of their women accept their fate unhesitatingly, but most of them gasp for freedom, and gradually reject the stereotype by going in for separation or for divorce to live a meaningful life. However, in the ultimate analysis both Sahgal and Lessing find that the tradition of family is very strong, and thus make a strong plea for the preservation of it, by inviting men to involve themselves in it.

(i) Status of Woman in Marriage

In her book *Women, Resistance and Revolution*, Sheila Rowbotham uses the term "colonialized" to show the oppressed status of women in the society. She cites "economic dependence," "cultural takeover" and "the identification of dignity with resemblance to the oppressor" as some of the "similarities that exist between the colonisation of the underdeveloped country and female oppression."[6] J.S. Mill is right in saying that marriage is the worst form of slavery for women. He says that "no slave is a slave to the same lengths, and in so full a sense of words, as a wife is."[7] Engels in his *The Origin of the Family* also points out that the Latin word *familia* means the total number of slaves belonging to one man. Marriage, he says, is not a "reconciliation of man and woman," but the subjugation of the female in the interest of perpetuation of slavery and the private property.

Marriage for a man who "takes her," means enlargement and confirmation of his existence. He enjoys both the worlds: of home and of career. It permits him progression and self-advancement. Since the woman is "given" in marriage, she become his "half" and takes his name, his religion, family and class. She is virtually reduced to the status of a "nurse-maid" or a "nanny" of the children. Before marriage, woman is made by her parents and after marriage, as Balzac puts it, "a wife is what her husband makes her."[8] She eventually finds, as Germaine Greer observes, that after marriage her life has "changed radically, but not her husband's."[9]

In her earlier works, Doris Lessing depicts marriage as an emotionally stifling and tyrannical institution for women. Most of her characters like Mary Turner, Martha, Maisie, Marjorie, Molly, Ella, Marion and Anna are victims of gender-oppression. However, most of these women refuse to accept the polarization of sexes. They do not want to define themselves in relation to men and hence seek identity and individuality in their own way. When they realize that they are being used and abused, they turn subversive of the tradition of being submissive and conforming persons, asserting their individuality and "consciousness" which are pre-requisites for women's liberation.

Throughout history, women have been appropriated as sexual objects. Karl Marx says, "*Marriage. . .* is incontestably a form of *exclusive private property*."[10]

Lessing's women resent men's sexist assumptions, viz., the stereotype images of women which define them primarily through their attraction or usefulness to men. In Lessing's *Martha Quest*, Martha does not want to be treated like a "sex-object" and feels offended when Donovan Anderson, her first boy-friend in the town, displays her before his friends. Donovan feels proud of his "acquisition" and makes her cynosure at sun-downer parties or cinema houses before the group of young "wolves" or "sharks" who try to get "girls in their grip."[11] Donovan finds Martha "a success" as the crowd of young men greatly admires her for her fresh looks. Martha feels a threat to her individuality and freedom which is followed by a "strong resisting dislike of his pressure on her." (157) She strongly resents the way Donovan "showed her off" (180) among his friends and decides to sever all relations with him.

In *A Proper Marriage,* Martha finds the same disgusting behaviour being repeated by her husband Douglas Knowell. Immediately after marriage, she is dragged from one party to another, where Douglas is repeatedly reminded for his good luck and "congratulated on his acquisition"[12] by his friends. Returning from a bar one night, he tells Martha people's opinion about her and endorses it too:

> "They think I'm a helluva lucky..." he announced; and at the thought of the scenes in the bar with the boys, a reflection of his proud and embarrassed grin appeared on his face. He swooped over to her, ground her tightly to him,, and announced, "And so – so I am." (34)

Martha, however, does not believe in becoming an object of "amusement" or "decoration" for her husband. She does not subscribe to the views held by her friend, Stella, that "It's your duty to your husband to look nice," (16) and disdains "female ruses" (96) played by women to keep their husbands under their thumb. She does not want to be known as a "paragon of beauty" and craves for no conventional praises like:

> Her cheeks lyke apples which the sun hath rudded,
> Her lips lyke cherryes charming men to byte,
> Her brest like to bowle of creame uncrudded.[13]

She wants to be recognized as a complete individual in her own right. To attain individuality and independence, Martha rejects this "feminine mystique" which glorifies only the physical beauty and utility of women. She does not want to be "applauded only with the hypocrisy of cheap sentiment."[14] Martha, further, does not want to identify herself with her husband or become merely an appendage to him. For that reason, she has no liking for Mrs. Maynard or Mrs. Talbot or women like them who enjoy the status and wealth of their husbands. She finds satisfaction in being "unique, individual and altogether apart from any other person," (31) a condition which is essential for achieving self-reliance. Martha, a seeker of freedom, feels concerned for the poor blacks in Rhodesia and joins the left group to help the oppressed. Marriage appears to be an encroachment on her "precious privacy" and she soon realizes that she has made a "foolish mistake" in getting married. She feels bored, "caged and trapped" as if "nets were tightening around her." (59) This awareness gradually leads her to a state of conflicting emotions which is aggravated by people's pressurizing influence on her to remain "properly married."

In *A Ripple from the Storm*, after her second marriage to Anton Hesse, Martha again feels uncomfortable and resentful because of the "possessiveness" in him. She again feels "caged and hemmed in."[15] This marriage also turns out to be a fiasco. Being a "free spirit," she finds comfort in the thought that she can revolt anytime against the tyrannies of "male authority."

However, Sahgal's women do not feel free to assert their individuality or defy the social institutions easily. The concept of woman as subservient to men (as preached by Manu), and as man's property is deep-rooted in Indian tradition as well. According to the popular myth, woman is *Paraya Dhan* whose custodians are her parents till the time she is handed over to her rightful owner, her husband. The husband in turn feels privileged to treat her as his personal property or his possession. Sahgal strongly condemns the attitudes which reduce woman to an object. Sahgal is not a staunch feminist and subscribes only "to the idea of it, though not to each and every aspect of it."[16] She confesses about feminist awakening in her: "I have come to this awakening rather late, although I have personally always been independent minded."[17] Nevertheless, her leaning towards liberal feminism is projected through her women characters who wish to combine marriage and their individuality in such a way that neither of them is harmed. Sometimes, contrary to the belief that "Hindu marriage is not a contract, it is a sacrament,"[18] some of her women act defiantly and sever the already splitting relations after giving sufficient time and thought to the delicate and sacred issue of marriage. Sahgal envisions marriage as a sweet harmonious relationship based on mutual understanding, depth and truth. "Women are persons not possessions" is the note echoed in all her works.

Like Lessing's Donovan or Douglas, Som in Sahgal's *The Day in Shadow* draws immense pleasure in showing off his wife as his "personal possession." He would often boast before his friends: "Look what I've got. Good enough to keep under lock and key."[19] Som treats his wife Simrit as a priceless object good enough for his personal pleasures. As a husband he is happy with the thought that his job is finished by adorning his wife with jewellery and fine expensive things. Simrit, however, finds the materialistic world of Som, consisting of beautiful and choicest clothes, jewels and trips abroad, quite meaningless. She only craves for some goal, some meaning beyond the world of self-advancement, a "world whose texture is kindly." (89) "Money," as Lionel Trilling says, "is the principle of the inauthentic in human existence."[20] Simrit, like Martha Knowell, finds the materialistic existence offered by her husband inauthentic and superficial, and a barrier to her self-realization. Martha Knowell in *A Proper Marriage* finds it difficult to cope with luxurious and comfortable existence on feudal pattern which her civil servant husband provides her. She longs for her independence away from hypocrisies, double standards and frivolities of the male-dominated society.

In Sahgal's *Storm in Chandigarh*, Inder believes that his wife Saroj "belongs" to him and is exclusively his "possession." Like a typical male chauvinist, he firmly believes:

> A thousand years from now a woman will still want and need a master, the man who will own and command her – and that's the man she'll respect.[21]

This sense of possessiveness and dictatorial attitude is natural for a man in patriarchy which grants "the father nearly ownership over wife or wives and children, including the powers of physical abuse and often even those of murder and sale. Classically, as head of the family, the father is both begetter and owner in a system in which kinship is property."[22]

(ii) Double Standards

Man considers it as normal male behaviour to satisfy his desires at both the emotional and the physical levels outside marriage, while it is ruthlessly condemned as adultery in case a woman indulges in it even though accidentally. At the slightest hint of any deviation on her part which may not even involve sex, man turns violent and hostile towards his wife and starts persecuting her. This condemnation is dictated by man's interest in preserving his property rather than by any moral consideration. Hardy in *Tess of the d'Urbervilles* and Nathaniel Hawthrone in *The Scarlet Letter* (to mention a few) have shown how women are persecuted and abandoned, whereas men are spared any punishment for the "sin" which is committed by both. While a traditional society insists on pre-marital virginity and marital chastity in women, men are allowed wide sexual liberty. These double standards are reflected in different practices allowing sexual liberties to men. Among the Hebrews and Semitic nomads, for the sexual freedom of men, "a special class of 'bad' women was created"[23] in the name of preserving the chastity of "good" women. Even now "prostitute houses" operate secretly for the benefit of men in all corners of the world. The "split between pronounced value and actual value, between what is said and what is done,"[24] is highly deplorable as it leads to constant discrimination against women.

In Sahgal's *Storm in Chandigarh*, Inder, the husband, who himself is hankering after another woman constantly rebukes and harasses his wife Saroj because of her past sexual indulgence with her college mate once. Inder is maddened by jealousy and behaves in a primitive manner by torturing her physically and mentally quite often. Several times in a day he would ask her about the "other" man and the number of times she has gone to bed with him, commenting that there must have been many others like "him" in her life. He ignores her several virtues and considers her "used, soiled and unfit for marriage," (96) all because of her one past act. One night, out of anger he almost strangles her for her "infidelity." Saroj thinks she has "committed no crime," (99) but Inder accepts no explanation nor does the society which thinks that "the one unpardonable crime for an unmarried girl is to have sexual intercourse with any man."[25] Ironically, Inder finds nothing wrong in his liaison with Mara while Saroj has been "branded sinner" by him. The husband has a social sanction to torture his wife on mere suspicion of her having sexual relations with another man; the wife on the other hand can do nothing to her husband if he behaves in a similar manner. She has no right to question her husband's fidelity. In this context one of Sahgal's characters makes a significant remark:

> If chastity is so important and so well worth preserving . . . it would be easier to safeguard it by keeping men in seclusion, not women. (191)

Sahgal feels that Saroj's pre-marital act of sex has nothing to do with the pollution of flesh, promiscuity or immorality. "The humanist in Nayantara champions for the new human values to blast its way through the jungle of superstition, pretence and seeming facade of politeness."[26]

Man in fact often takes pride in his extra-marital involvements. Ram Swarup, for example, in *Rich Like Us* has already two wives at home, Mona and Rose, but he continues to develop ardent love affairs. When he is involved with Marcella, he does not at all take care to hide it from Rose to save her from being hurt. Rather he comes home with "his footfall open and normal on the stair at three a.m." (94) There is no communication between Ram and Rose for four months but to her it seems she has been suffering for years: "Her anguish and rage fought for an outlet and gathered like a gale inside her without a word said." (94) Earlier Mona was suffering because of Ram's love for Rose and now Rose also suffers in the same manner. But like Mona, Rose is equally helpless to do anything and "in the utter stillness the thin sobbing sound of pure grief no one was meant to hear, froze Mona's tears in Rose's eyes." (94)

Lessing the champion of women's freedom, does not advocate sexual liberty for women as such but finds nothing wrong in relationships based on mutual love and respect. In an interview, Lessing once remarked furiously:

> I'm impatient with people who emphasize sexual revolution. I say we should all go to bed, shut up about sexual liberation, and go on with the important matters.[27]

It is in fact emotional fulfilment rather than sexual freedom that is the main issue. In Lessing's *The Golden Notebook*, the men who come to Anna and Ella are all married with wives at home to look after children while they look for sex, love and fulfilment outside marriage. Even in the permissive western society, the wife 's sexual freedom is unacceptable and leads to her persecution and torture. In *A Proper Marriage,* Douglas doubts his wife's fidelity and turns violent towards her. He treats her brutally when he learns that Martha has been mixing with Air Force men in his absence during war. In order to occupy herself in some constructive work, Martha has joined "Help for Our Allies Committee," where she comes across an active member of the group, William. She is drawn towards him and openly moves around with him in Douglas's absence. Douglas feels that Martha is ignoring him and their daughter Caroline for the sake of her lover and is filled with jealousy. He expresses his anger by physically abusing her, grabbing her wrist and twisting it. One night when she comes late after attending a meeting of the group, he loses his temper and pounces upon Martha:

> "Tell me, Martha – did you sleep with him, did you?"
> "No, I didn't."
> He repeated it; she repeated it. She fell off to sleep again. Again she woke up in the dark, to hear that persistent voice, this time repeating, "Did you sleep with Hesse?"
> She laughed. "No, don't be absurd."
> He went through a list of names. (351)

Martha is aware that Douglas too had been involved in "dozens of love affairs" (190) at his place of posting. But being a woman, she has no right to question her husband's fidelity. Like Sahgal, Lessing attacks double standards, jealousies and opportunism in marriage and finds these tendencies destructive for harmonious relationships.

In *The Golden Notebook,* Paul is jealous of his mistress Ella and accuses her of having relations with other men. He uses the phrase "your literary lunches"[28] for her infidelities, and often accuses her of making eyes at men whom she in fact "has not even noticed." (212) While having an affair with Ella, Paul not only has his wife at home but is also having another affair simultaneously with a colleague, Stephanie, and yet he is jealous and suspicious of Ella's affairs. As far as his wife is concerned he is totally immune to her emotional needs, who is no more to him than an instrument of delivering and nurturing babies. Not only wives, men want to cut their mistresses also completely to their requirements and always find fault in them. Paul has almost abandoned his mute, docile and homely wife Muriel to sleep with his "smart gay, sexy mistress" Ella. When Ella puts on simple clothes, he tells her that she looks like a "severe school mistress" and when she switches over to revealing clothes, low cut blouses etc., he becomes jealous of her smart seductive looks. Man wants his woman to be vigorous, healthy and chaste for him but cold to others. He considers "sexual pleasures" as a male privilege and woman's claim to it arouses male-anger, and he generally repudiates feminine sensuality. Simone de Beauvoir very effectively brings out the unfortunate state of women in marriage: "It is the duplicity of the husband that dooms the wife to a misfortune of which he complains later that he is himself the victim. Just as he wants her to be at once warm and cool in bed, he requires her to be wholly his and yet no burden; he wishes her to establish him in a fixed place on earth and to leave him free, to assume the monotonous daily round and not to bore him, to be always at hand and never importunate; he wants to have her all to himself and not to belong to her; to live as one of the couple and to remain alone. Thus she is betrayed from the day he marries her."[29]

Lessing further exposes the double standards, the callousness, hypocrisies and indifference of men against women in *The Golden Notebook* very impressively. Richard, after leaving his first wife Molly and son Tommy, marries Marion and has three children from this marriage. Still he seeks pleasure with his secretaries and has a "succession of girls." He treats Marion like a housewife or a hostess for his posh dinner parties, never as a human being who also needs man's love and affection for sustaining herself. She is virtually reduced to the status of a "nursemaid for the children" (278) and occupies a "position as prisoner" (376) in her home. When Marion complains about his girls, Richard asks her to have a lover. And when a man does get interested in her and is ready to marry her with all the three children, Richard becomes jealous. Richard's first wife Molly lashes out at him for treating Marion as a "stupid and insensitive woman" (49) and for his hypocrisies:

> "You were worried about her being unhappy?" said Molly, laughing contemptuously. "No, your vanity was hurt. You worked really hard to make her in love with you again, it was all jealous scenes and love and kisses until that moment she broke it off with him finally. And the moment you had her safe, you lost interest and went back to the secretaries on the fancy divan in your beautiful big business office. And you think it's so unjust that Marion is unhappy and makes scenes and drinks more than is good for her." (48)

When out of frustration Marion starts drinking, Richard accuses her of being a "bad influence on the children." (48) And when she ceases to drink and devotes her energy to looking after her stepson, Tommy, who has become blind due to a suicidal attempt, Richard feels wounded and blames her for not caring for him: "She has no time for me." (376) In fact, he is making lame excuses to abandon her and marry his twenty-three-year old secretary Jane, which would be his third marriage, that too when he is already fifty.

Marriage turns into a trap, an institution of oppression and torment for women. Richard, Douglas or Inder, all are male chauvinists who rule their women with a very stern and stringent set of rules while themselves enjoying all the freedom. They use and abuse women as objects and their personal possessions and try to crush their "self" in order to enslave them.

(iii) Violence and Loneliness

The basis for a happy and harmonious marriage is the feeling of sharing, equality and true partnership. But in the patriarchal division of values, equality is not possible because all the superior and positive qualities are attributed to men and the qualities associated with women are considered to be inferior. Helene Cixous has given some examples of binary oppositions corresponding to the underlying oppositions of man/woman such as:

Activity/ Passivity
Sun/Moon
Culture/Nature
Day/Night
Father/Mother
Head/Emotions
Intelligible/Sensitive
Logos/Pathos.[30]

These oppositions are thoroughly imbricated in the patriarchal value system, where the feminine side is always seen as negative and a source of darkness.

Lynne Segal believes that "men wield power over women through terror."[31] Man evokes fear in the mind of women by his superior muscular power and by extreme emotional indifference and callousness which make woman so vulnerable. Woman suffers not only by man's act of physical violence, but she is often emotionally hurt and crippled through his arrogance, cynicism and indifference. He never admires his wife's services and sacrifices for the family and takes them as guaranteed by the institution of marriage. She is belittled or silenced, and denied love, friendship and togetherness in marriage. Man longs only for his own *raison d'etre;* woman's needs have no meaning for him. Simone de Beauvoir says that for "loyalty and friendship" to exist between man and woman, the essential condition is that they should be "free in relation to each other and be equal on concrete matters."[32] However, man thinks that woman is everything negative that he is not, and behaves accordingly. This blocks the road to the communication between the partners in marriage. The "communication gap" is ruinous for the institution of marriage. "Dialogue" or "discussion" is essential for harmonious marital relationship. The need for "talk" or "dialogue" is very much stressed in Sahgal's works. Due to lack of "communication"[33] and mutual understanding, a large number of Sahgal's characters suffer from the private torment of broken marriages. The spouses live together under the same roof, still they experience emptiness, loneliness and alienation. It is not physical loneliness that Sahgal talks of, but deeper emotional and spiritual voids created by egoism. Her characters have an "empty shell" marriage, defined by sociologist as the marriage "where the spouses live together, remain legally married but their marriage exists in name only."[34] On the surface, her couples seem to be happy and contented, but they often experience loneliness and complain of silences in marriage, as Saroj in *Storm in Chandigarh* laments: "It's not being alone I mind – I enjoy that. It's the loneliness. I'm alone even when Inder is here." (223) Not only Saroj, but her husband Inder equally feels lonely and craves for companionship outside marriage. He finds Mara (Jit's wife) more friendly and shares his intimate thoughts with her. Saroj wants to bridge the widened gap and live "without pretence" but Inder remains hard and cold, mainly because of Saroj's past. Jasbir Jain believes that there is something "within him which shuts her out, and is impervious to her affection. He on his part treats her merely as a wife and not as a person."[35] It is his ego and his sense of superiority that stands in the way of sharing and caring. Saroj's quest for communication and sharing naturally leads her towards Vishal, whom she finds more understanding and considerate. Inder, a sadist, never approves of his wife's overtures and turns violent towards her. He finds no meaning in Saroj's fervent pleas for sharing: "After all, we are so unlike, and it's natural we should need friends who share our interests." (20) The problem with Inder is that like Richard in *The Golden Notebook* he neither loves his wife, nor does he want that she should be loved by any other man.

Another couple in the novel, Jit and Mara, have "no intimacies except in bed." (232) Their marriage according to Hindu tradition was an arranged one and decided hurriedly. In retrospection, Mara remembers how marriage came to her when she was "young and desire was ripe and easy to confuse with the most complicated need called love." (100) Mara is blessed with all the worldly comforts from life, i.e beauty, wealth and social status but she suffers from emotional void in her life. The search for communication makes her come towards Inder. She requests him to "meet more and get to know each other." (171) But soon she is disillusioned when she finds him a hypocrite, and breaks all relations with him. By that time Jit also realizes that there is something lacking in their relationship and makes an attempt to come closer to her. Through the effective use of an epiphany, Sahgal describes the moment when a sense of sudden radiance and revelation comes to Mara and she immediately decides to resume her life with Jit happily and meaningfully:

> Strength that was almost physical in its impact reached out to her in his words, the kind of strength she had never thought she would need as she went her proud way alone.
>
> She said what she had never been able to say before, "I need your help." (233)

The realization makes them be reconciled and remain true to each other. After that there is a likelihood that their relationship will be more genuine and fuller and not merely a matter of surfaces as in the case of Saroj and Inder.

Discussing the importance of "talk" or communication in human relationship, Rollo May, a psycho-therapist, observes:

> Communication recovers the original "we-ness" of the human being on a new level... one relates to another not as receptacle for the expression of one's own sexuality, or as a being to be exploited for assuaging of one's loneliness, or in any other way as an object, but as a human being in the full meaning of that term. Communicating leads to community—that is to understanding, intimacy, and the mutual valuing that was previously lacking.[36]

In *The Day in Shadow*, "talk was the missing link" (93) between Som and Simrit, ultimately causing breakdown of their seventeen-year-old wedlock. Som, a "damned good husband," (89) a wealthy business man, leaves no stone unturned to keep Simrit happy with worldly objects and even suggests her that "we can go abroad anytime we want, any bloody time, buy anything we want. We can air-condition this whole place, furnish it, all over again." (89) He, however, never tries to understand the reasons for his sensitive, intelligent wife's unhappiness, who only wants to talk to him: a "good talk, about books, events, ideas, people" (93) or anything else which is "shared" by her husband. During the course of conversation with his friends, she is, however, deliberately kept out. Som and his friend would talk endlessly "to each other in Punjabi in her presence, ignoring her. But Som would squeeze and stroke her arm, rest his hand warmly, heavily on her thigh, keep her physically in the room, mentally out." (27) Both the friends would share their memories of pre-partition days of India; how they were uprooted and so on, but they "did not look at her" during their discussion, thus giving immense mental torture to Simrit who always wanted to be a part of them. They would never discuss business details in her presence as if it was something "obsence and unmentionable, or women were morons – she wasn't sure which – so most of Som stayed cut off from her. Her usefulness to him had never extended to the areas of the mind." (77) For an educated and sensitive woman like Simrit, her husband's indifference is extremely inhuman, particularly when she wholeheartedly desires deeper relationship. Like Saroj, Simrit often does not feel the presence of Som, even though physically he is with her. She recalls the experience she once had during the long drive along the Beas:

> "This drive along the Beas, you shared it with Som, didn't you?"
> "Oh God no. I sat in the car with him, that was all." (36)

Talking about loneliness in human relationship, Germaine Greer says: "many a housewife staring at the back of her husband's newspaper, or listening to his breathing in bed is lonelier than any spinster in a rented room."[37] Most of Sahgal's women suffer in marriage because their men like to remain "locked up in their solitary cells"[38] and do not try to reach them. They do not recognize the fact that love is necessary to happiness and "the closer together people get, the more independent and self-contained their relation becomes."[39]

In *Rich Like Us*, Ram inflicts great emotional violence on both the women he marries. He sees every relationship in life in terms of his own advantage and gratification. Insensitive to the feelings of his first wife Mona, he brings an English wife Rose after Mona has given birth to Ram's son. Rose in turn has to suffer humiliation, and hostility in the house as she is looked upon as an "intruder," and sometimes she herself starts feeling guilty. Ironically wronged by a man both the women start resenting each other. While Mona tries to hurt Rose by frequently reminding her that she (i.e. Mona) is the mistress of the house, Rose in her heart of hearts starts wishing for the death of Mona, foolishly hoping that everything will be all right after Mona's death.

The traditional wife that she is, Mona in spite of the injustice done to her keeps on fasting and praying for husband's long life, but often her "loud insistent tears" (41) are heard by Rose who lives on the upper floor. Rose is filled with "a rebellious active misery" (53) and also with a sense of insecurity when Ram often gets up from his bed and goes down to soothe his wailing wife Mona and then remains with her for hours and sometimes for the whole night. When Rose does not make any effort to communicate her suffering to Ram, he just ignores her agony by turning the whole issue into a joke. Rose tells Ram:

"I don't think I can take much more of this, Ram."
"Of what?" he had the temerity to ask.
"You living with two wives."
He was stretched out on his bed, too good-humoured and too lazy to quarrel.
"Lord Krishna had three hundred." (54)

While Ram refers to *Ramayana* and *Mahabharta* to justify his bigamy, Rose on the contrary is struck with the character of Sita. Sita repeatedly figures in the narrative as the archetype of the wronged woman, and Rose at various crucial moments in her life thinks of Sita.

Instead of love, self-gratification becomes the basis of marriage for man and he usually deprives woman of togetherness and warmth. The denial of love can make her deviate from the norms sometimes. Sahgal deals with "anomie"[40] in human situation in *This Time of Morning* and holds the husband responsible for the anomic behaviour of his wife. Arjun Mitra, a top bureaucrat with a western background, at the age of thirty-three marries a young beautiful, nineteen-year-old girl Uma. The brilliant, responsible, and successful officer, however, remains absorbed in his officialdom. Climbing the ladder of success, he forgets that in Uma "marriage had released a torrent of hungry sensuousness that brought to startling focus her exotic feline beauty." (26) Marriage has made her "bored and idle" and she longs for his love and company. But Arjun remains oblivious of her physical and sensual needs and expects her to take interest in the library and neighbourhood or "share his life" of books and ideas. He is very sensitive to the rumours circulating about her, the knowledge of which makes him behave like a stranger to her. Instead of caring for her needs he "condemned himself to an isolation where she could never reach or touch him again." (28) "Uma was dead" (28) for him though he continues to provide her with food, shelter and the protection of his name. His indifferent behaviour makes her so desperate emotionally and sexually that she takes to drinking and moving alone with men, deviating from the social norms. On several occasions during official parties, Uma disappears with any man who flirts with her a little to satisfy her physical thirsts, unmindful of "public humiliation" (166) she may have to face on account of her conduct. In a party given by Rani of Mirpur, a South American finds her very "exquisite" and sensual and drinks to her eyes. When they are alone in a room, "she neither encouraged nor discouraged him. She let his hand take hers, slide up her arm, go round her waist. Her headache receded slightly and she felt relief in his skill and deftness.... It was complete in itself and needed no explanation." (109) On another occasion, Arjun finds her in a room in a hotel with another foreigner, Neil Berensen, the architect of Peace Institute. Entering Neil's room (No. 420: the number itself is suggestive of corruption), Arjun finds "Neil's tie on a chair, his shirt sleeves, the faint smear of lipstick on his mouth.... For here he was forced to be witness to her unspeakable behaviour." (166) The scene speaks of the frustration and dissatisfaction in Uma's life. Marriage has made this loving innocent girl, a wild "tigress in a meadow." (26) Sahgal herself says that through Uma's character she wants to say that a "woman is not allowed to be a woman in orthodox thinking. She has to be 'good' and good means virtuous in the sense of chaste. Uma was a woman with appetites that her husband couldn't satisfy, so she indulged them elsewhere. Men do it, and there's no comment."[41]

Contrasted with the character of Uma is Maya in *A Time to be Happy.* Maya is the wife of a well-to-do Deputy Collector and, like Uma, she is also childless. In her marital relationship she also needs a response, just a "response" of any kind, which she fails to get from her husband. Unlike Uma she does not become anomic, but joins India's freedom movement and preaches Gandhian ideology to simple villagers, and tries to seek self-fulfilment in this role.

Sahgal has shown her male characters mostly as narrow-minded, ruthless, careless husbands who make their sensitive wives experience acute sense of loneliness, emptiness, and boredom in life. However, exceptionally though, her male characters equally suffer in a wrong marriage, due to loneliness or lack of communication. They may not undergo the same kind of agony because man is not dependent in the same way as his wife is on him, but a wrong marriage gives him a lot of torture too. Vishal in *Storm in Chandigarh* suffers because there is no communication and understanding between him and his wife Leela who lives like a "stranger to him." (217) She is rather carrying on a secret affair with another man, Hari. When Vishal demands the truth in order to help her in the matter, she flatly denies having any sort of intimacy with him, thus leaving no scope for reconciliation.

A similar discord can be seen in the married life of Usman and Nadira in *A Situation in New Delhi*. Usman, a Vice-Chancellor, is over-burdened with the troubles of unrest, violence, rape in the University Campus and also with the changing socio-political situation in the country after the death of the patriotic leader Shivraj. Usman desires whole-heartedly to share his deepest and innermost thoughts with Nadira, but the latter remains stubborn, uncompromising, and refuses to come out of the fortress around her. Nadira, who is much younger to Usman, has accepted marriage in terms of physical union only and feels unconcerned with his emotional burden. However, their splitting relationship is saved from further break-up by the "will to understand" and like Jit and Mara in *Storm in Chandigarh,* there is a hope of fuller and deeper relationship.

Marriage often makes the aware and sensitive women very unhappy and discontented. Marriage makes Rashmi in *This Time of Morning* "a moth trapped in cement." (35) When Rakesh, her childhood friend, meets Rashmi after a long interval, he finds that she has changed profoundly and "looked displaced." (35) He is sure that it is marriage that had altered this once happy and lively girl. Rashmi has "suffered the wilderness that only two mismatched people could create" (123) in marriage. Despite her efforts to "endure, reconcile and preserve," (13) she was caught in a labyrinth of despair and disappointments. Remembering her agonies, she now thinks: "How like prolonged starvation wrong marriage could be, robbing lustre, defeating courage and will." (13) A contemporary of Sahgal, Kamala Markandaya talks of hunger and starvation in her *A Handful of Rice*. Sahgal's characters are well-fed and financially quite secure in their lives, and yet they suffer because of a more acute hunger – emotional starvation in marriage.

Loneliness, suffering and frustration in marriage sometimes cause disintegration and make some women even schizophrenic as Mary in Lessing's *The Grass is Singing*. The novel is a poignant portrayal of Mary's disintegration and death because of her unhappy marriage. Mary, an independent, poised and amiable woman who disdains the very idea of marriage, is hastened into wedlock, after the malicious remarks made by her own friends who conform to the view that marriage is "the sole justification of her (a woman's) existence."[42] In Mary's case, it is not the possessiveness, jealousy or cruelty of a man but mismatching which is responsible for tragedy. After a hurried courtship, before they could understand and know the likes and dislikes of each other, Mary marries Dick who also needs her solely to fight his own loneliness. Loneliness is the only common point between the two, who have otherwise different pasts, different experiences and different backgrounds. While Mary "loved the town, felt safe there,"[43] Dick dislikes the town-culture. Being a farmer, he loves spending most of his time on his farm. After marriage also, Dick remains busy in his farm work, going in the morning, returning late in the evening and retiring to bed immediately after supper.

The sexual relationship of Mary and Dick is not very satisfactory from the beginning. While Dick unintentionally makes her a "sexual object by idealizing her, Mary can only accept him when he approaches her submissively.

Then yielding to him in a martyr-like way expecting outrage and imposition, she was relieved to find she felt nothing."[44] Thus even sex does not bring them any closer, it rather separates them. Mary realizes that motherhood can give her some happiness and fulfilment, and at one stage she talks to Dick about having a child but Dick refuses on account of his poverty, which in fact is caused largely by his own failures and stubbornness. Now Mary tries to find meaning in life by sewing, stitching and mending "as if fine embroidery would save her life." (65) The gulf between the two, however, keeps on widening and in their small, lonely home "they were stunted, unfulfilled figures."[45] Marriage closes doors for her for any career as well. The woman, who was once admired and loved by the society is disqualified because of her sloppy appearance and unpolished manners. She comes back and ultimately resigns herself to the traditional role of a woman, i.e. of looking after her home and husband.

Later, Mary is gradually drawn towards her Black servant, Moses, who looks after her tenderly when she falls ill. Moses fulfils her need for warmth, care and communication which Dick has failed to provide. But then Moses kills her in the end when she is leaving the farm for good. He probably thinks that she is deserting him.

While Lessing's Mary disintegrates, and becomes schizophrenic, her other women do not necessarily break down; rather they prefer to continue their search for individuality and self-realization. Martha's quest for identity and individuality (which began in *Martha Quest*) continues after her marriage to Douglas Knowell, when she realizes what marriage means for a woman – it threatens her identity and thwarts her pursuit of self-realization and self-actualization. The novel opens after Martha's wedding to Douglas which immediately leads her to reflect on men, marriage and motherhood.

Douglas is Martha's own choice and unlike Mary in *The Grass is Singing*, she is not pressurised by the society to marry. But soon she discovers her incompatibility with Douglas and articulates her dissatisfaction: "I haven't anything in common with Douglas, and I've been unhappy all the time." (353) She fails to understand as to why she married in the first place, as "she did not feel at all identified with her husband or his circle" (52) – the gang of "boys," who love their own world of sundowners, bars, dances and dinners rather than their homes. And when the Second World War is announced, these "boys" feel as if "they were soldiers. They returned to their women late in the evening, cheerful strangers." (150) Martha finds the "atmosphere of men escaping their wives" quite "intolerable." (151) Martha and her friends Stella and Alice also realize that their "men preferred other company to theirs," and hence feel lonely and even "wished they had never married, and wished they were not pregnant, even hated their husbands." (152) These intelligent, enterprising women do not want to be "stuck at home." They feel encaged and enslaved and are suffering from "boredom, the tedium of living alone, the unsatisfactory nature of marriage, the burden of bringing up children" (234) etc. Since it is war time, they encourage their husbands to save their country at the cost of their happiness. Martha "sets no bounds" (96) on Douglas and never questions his activities like a good companion and a friend. When Douglas's turn comes to reciprocate, he crushes her wish to join Red Cross Course. Martha is exposed to male hypocrisy which makes even "intelligent and liberal-minded men lapse back into the anonymous voice of authority whenever their own personal authority is threatened, saying things of a banality and a pomposity infinitely removed from their own level of thinking." (106-7) Douglas's indifference and selfishness enhance the loneliness of Martha's life and she finds herself "doomed to the continuation of the species and the care of the home."[46] Marriage, instead of freeing her from loneliness, makes her more lonely, insecure and unhappy. Though Douglas does his best to keep her satisfied with material comforts, Martha feels "fed-up" and "bored" (295) with her false, pretentious, empty and meaningless existence. The "instinct to comply, to please, seemed to her more and more unpleasant and fake." (292) She rejects her mother's suggestion to uphold the traditional values and remain "properly married." (353) Unlike Mary who breaks down in the face of sufferings, Martha refuses to accept marriage as a career. While she revolts against parental authority in *Martha Quest*, in *A Proper Marriage* she frees herself from the fold of marriage by seeking a divorce in search of her own identity and self.

In *A Ripple from the Storm*, Martha is further disillusioned. She is exposed to male jealousy, when William with whom she has a short affair is posted out because of pressure on the camp authorities by Douglas, who thinks that Martha has left him and Caroline for this Air Force Sergeant. William tells her that he will take "legal advice" in the matter, which makes Martha realize that he is no better than Douglas. She "understood that he was enjoying the idea of fight with Douglas over the possession of her – then, for a few moments, she had seen the two men as one, and identical with the pompous, hypocritical and essentially male fabric of society." (25) The announcement of William's departure, hence, relieves her a lot.

One observes the growth of Martha's character from the personal to the political as Martha involves herself in the activities of the communist group and works for the upliftment of the poor, oppressed, black *Kaffirs*. She "becomes violently pro-native and attempts anything that will lead to substantial personal values."[47] Her intellectual friendship with a dedicated member of the group, Anton Hesse, turns into their marriage. However, she observes that "a new personality had been born in Anton with the marriage," (239) that he is not a mature, composed and integrated person he pretended to be. Martha discovers that their ideas on most matters do not coincide. She finds that he has compartmentalized his life into various parts, and gives more importance to the communist group above others. The sexual side of her marriage is full of disappointments. However, she never expresses it to Anton, and remains kind, loving and caring towards him. She learns that Anton had deceived her by hiding the truth of his first marriage with Grete, whose memories always haunt him and he constantly discusses her with Martha. Martha longs for wholeness, closeness, depth and truth in her relationship with Anton, but he treats her "as if she did not exist." (273) It is not a marriage at all for Martha, and she decides that once the war is over "we will go our ways." (247) Martha cherishes companionship, affection and respect in her conjugal relationship, but its reciprocity is repeatedly denied to her. Consequently she is gradually drawn towards Thomas and develops extra-marital relations with him.

Extra-marital relations are no solution to the marital problems, though these give some stability to a disjointed life sometimes. It is only love, candour, consent, companionship and tenderness within marriage itself, which can save marriage from disintegration and dissolution. However, a large number of Lessing's women who develop extra-marital relationships do it not out of sexual greed but to fulfil their longing for companionship, togetherness, tenderness and affection which they often miss in their conjugal relationship. As Eric Berne feels, "companionship is a twosome and may or may not involve in sex. Companions usually have a certain amount of respect and affection for each other."[48]

In her essay on "Adultery in Life and Literature," Sahgal also observes that if desire for love and truth leads people to extra-marital relations, there is nothing wrong or condemnable in it. She says:

> What is right and what is wrong? What should we do or not do? Perhaps both in India and in the permissive West the deciding factor before we act, or judge the actions of others, should be the aesthetics of a particular situation. Is it guided by love and aspiration or greed and gluttony? Is there truth and beauty in it or only the desire for gain?[49]

Though Sahgal's women are not so articulate, free and frank about sexual matters as Lessing's women are, yet they react to the suffering caused by loneliness, non-communication and incompatibility in a defiant manner. Saroj in *Storm in Chandigarh* lacks moral courage to break her painful marital bondage. With the help of an understanding companion, Vishal, she finally overcomes her initial hesitations and comes out of her husband's home. Simrit in *The Day in Shadow* leaves Som after seventeen years of unhappy married life. However, Rashmi in *This Time of Morning* makes a quick decision in the matter, leaves her husband and comes to stay with her parents. She has a short affair with a foreigner, Neil Berensen, but her desire for a deeper relationship remains unsatisfied again. She later finds Rakesh more loving and understanding and there is a possibility of an opening here.

In the patriarchal set-up, marriage divides power in favour of man. Man himself may not be so bad, but once a husband he behaves differently and demands total subservience from the wife. Thus, it is the institution of marriage which does more harm and makes man possessive, arrogant and violent. In *The Golden Notebook*, after divorce Richard develops a friendly attitude towards his former wife Molly and quite often seeks her help in his domestic matters. When, tortured by Richard, his second wife Marion takes to too much drinking, Richard requests Molly and her friend Anna to persuade her to stop drinking.

Man is not necessarily evil in Sahgal also. Outside marriage the power division is not there, hence usually man and woman meet as two individuals, not as the ruler and the ruled. Hence, they have a more satisfying relationship. But in marriage, men are always demanding and expecting more without giving anything. No wonder, Sahgal's Saroj, Simrit and Rashmi feel happy and satisfied with their friends, Vishal, Raj and Rakesh respectively.

(iv) Attitude to Love and Marriage

Love, in fact, is the essential need of Lessing's women. Most of her women marry and remarry not because they want to gratify their sexual urges but because they strive for love in the form of understanding, sharing and participation. But in a male-dominated society, as Friedan observes, "Love has customarily been defined, at least for women, as a complete merging of egos and a loss of separateness – 'togetherness,' a giving up of individuality rather than a strengthening of it."[50] While woman is supposed to completely give up her individuality in love as well as in marriage, for man these mean self-gratification on all fronts.

Sex is "essentially emotional" for women as Ella puts it in *The Golden Notebook*. In women "sex hunger" arises out of "emotional hunger." She cannot enjoy sex unless she loves the man. The men portrayed by Lessing are largely incurable womanizers, as rakes having a number of mistresses or "keeps." Despite their marriage, they are involved in a number of affairs which is a matter of *a la mode* for them. In *The Golden Notebook* Paul Tanner, bored with his wife, spends his nights with Ella at her place and the arrangement continues for several years. When Ella responds to the warmth of his relationship and when she cannot imagine living without him, he frees her, as he puts it, for "other boy-friends." (208) He manages to get a job in Nigeria, in order to get rid of her, and leaves Ella most callously. Ella lives in constant agony because she had started depending completely on Paul for her own happiness. Similarly Anna and Michael have a long affair stretched over four years, but finally Michael breaks it off, and leaves her for another woman when Anna has started loving him deeply and cannot bear the idea of staying alone.

Ella's colleague Patricia was also abandoned by her husband who "left her for a younger woman." (208) Men carefully keep their wives and children in their country homes and have "sex-adventures" at their bachelor flats, as does an editor friend of Ella. Men do not want to give anything in "return." (481) The plots of several stories of Anna, the writer, revolve round these themes in the novel (515-525): infidelity is a trait common to all men and they are utterly indifferent to the emotions of the woman they live with, be it wife or mistress. These sketches for short stories, which are based on Anna's own experience and observation of men, repeatedly reveal that the attitude of man towards love is highly selfish and detached. For a man, love is a matter of casual *affair d'amour*. Love for him is a temporary "refuge" from boredom and loneliness. For a woman, love means complete emotional involvement with the man. She wants lasting and stable relationship and permanence. Man looks upon sex as a means of self-gratification and sensual pleasures whereas woman relates it to the emotional fulfilment and meaning in life.

Another character in the novel, George, is a "sensualist," and when he "looked at a woman he was imagining her as she would be when he had fucked her into insensibility." (137) George always needs a woman to be under his "spell physically." Even though he is married and has children, he is carrying on an affair with a Black woman Marie, and has a child from this union, but his "sex-adventure" is never-ending. Man regards the act of love as a service rendered to him and for all the comfort and pleasures he gets from the wife, he thinks he owes her only food and shelter.

In most cases, both in Lessing's and Sahgal's works, after the birth of children, man ceases to love his wife and flirts around. He needs his wife when he is weak or sick, or in old age to "fulfil the function of kindly nannies or nursemaids." (521) He is not obliged to marry his mistress and carries on his overtures as long as he needs sex, and when the woman expreses her desire for security and lasting relationship, he leaves her in the lurch. Man is always demanding, and does not want to give anything in return. He is eager to take, not to exchange. Thus, for woman love means only giving and bestowing herself emotionally and physically, suppressing her own needs wholly; for man it is fulfilment of all his needs, sexual and emotional.

While woman always tries to "bolster-up" man, encourage him by covering up his weakness, he treats her as the other. He constantly blames her and projects his own infirmities on woman. Whereas she gives him confidence, he criticizes her for faults which are not even hers. Anna and Ella find that Jack and Americans like Maitland and Nelson and many others who come to them for "more sex" leaving behind their beautiful, attractive wives are themselves sexually crippled, but they instead accuse their wives of being frigid and cold. While the women give them support, "build" and "create" them, they criticize them for "being castrating," (470) etc. Men are polygamous by nature, women are monogamous. The revealing discussion between Martha and Thomas in *The Landlocked* sums up the attitude of men: "Well, there's only one thing for women, they have to stay married to one man and stay faithful, no matter what their husbands do." (122) Men are basically, as Lessing comments, "bullies and betrayers, but particularly . . . underminers and sappers."[51]

Love is merely fun or at the most passion for Sahgal's Ram Swarup in her *Rich Like Us.* Here Sahgal deals with the question of bigamy which entails sufferings and sacrifices for the co-wives, Mona and Rose. Both of them are wronged by a man for whom age is no barrier for love-affairs. Despite his two marriages, he is infatuated with Marcella, a young beautiful British lady, and falls deeply in love with her. So much so, he gets separation from Rose for Marcella's sake. The separation, however, does not work for a long time and ultimately it is Rose (since Mona is already dead) who looks after him tenderly after he is paralayzed. In her first novel *A Time to be Happy,* Sahgal has hinted at the issue of bigamy, where Harilal Mathur marries twice but his first wife submits to her fate without grumbling. Ram starts courting Rose in England right at the time when he gets the news of the birth of a son from his first wife. Neither the duty towards wife nor the thoughts of the newly-born child can stop Ram from showering his time and gifts and love on Rose till he finally wins her heart, and returns to India with his second wife. Life for both the women means insecurity and agony, while for Ram it is a profitable arrangement on all the fronts. As his friend Zafar remarks, "You have the path to heaven all paved for you . . . with a cocktail party upstairs and a prayer meeting downstairs." (65) Ram enjoys life fully with both the wives, with Mona looking after the household and the child and Rose providing sensual pleasure and a company in business, whereas both the women feel wronged, lonely and insecure. But he is not content even with these two. He turns to Marcella for an ardent love affair without any feeling of guilt and without caring for the feeling of his wives. He separates from Rose for the sake of Marcella. Later when the plan of living with Marcella does not materialize, he as easily asks Rose to come back and stay in the same house with him (for his business convenience), without even offering an apology or explanation for his behaviour. Since Rose is emotionally dependant on him, he can easily exploit her. In fact, he always takes his wives for granted and just goes ahead with whatever he feels like doing. Later he turns to the wife of the First Secretary in the Belgian embassy and gets so involved with her that he has no time to go to see Mona who is suffering from cancer and does not have long to live. Not only love, even marriage has no power to bind man to the woman. Marriage for man means getting all the comforts at every level while for woman it means a life of total dedicated service to a master.

(v) Woman and Motherhood

The feminists who reject the institution of marriage also discourage motherhood. They find it another form of slavery, as it breaks woman's self-sufficiency. They argue that with the coming of children, woman depends much more on man economically and emotionally. She remains subordinate to him and her position becomes more vulnerable on becoming a mother. Juliet Mitchell observes that it is within the "role as mother and housekeeper that woman finds the oppression that is hers alone."[52]

Traditionally, motherhood is regarded as the "biological destiny" and the greatest ambition of a woman. A child is considered to be woman's happiness and her justification, through which she is supposed to find self-fulfilment and self-realization. In India, woman's identity and her well-being depend on her producing a child, especially a male child. Swami Vivekanand glorified motherhood in these words:

> The ideal of womanhood in India is motherhood – that marvellous, unselfish, all-suffering, ever forgiving mother. The wife walks behind

> the shadow. She must imitate the life of the mother; that is her duty. But the mother is the ideal of life, she rules the family, she possesses the family.[53]

However, contrary to these glorious assertions, motherhood proves to be a suffocating experience for most of Sahgal's and Lessing's women. Sahgal's Simrit and Lessing's Anna, Molly and Ella sacrifice themselves to bring up their children all by themselves, but even their progeny often add to their suffering. Simrit in *The Day in Shadow*, after divorce, does her best to bring up their children. When the son Brij grows up, Som, the father, tempts him with luxurious goods, viz. a record player, a car etc., and promises to send him abroad too. He succeeds in his strategy and gets the custody of the boy. Instead of becoming a support to the mother the grown-up son too prefers to live with his father to enjoy a more comfortable and luxurious life. Germaine Greer rightly observes that a woman has no right on her children: "the children are not *hers*, they are not her property."[54] In a patriarchal society, the male child is always preferred as he perpetuates the father's name. Som does not take the daughters back because daughters mean a lot of expenditure in terms of their dowry at the time of their marriage. Hence he leaves the daughters for his estranged wife to look after, who is already struggling under the financial burden of a brutal divorce settlement. Even when women are free from the bondage of marriage, a child becomes a new bondage.

Lessing's Molly in *The Golden Notebook*, after divorce from Richard, brings up her son, Tommy, as a single parent, sacrificing her ambitions and desires. In return, she too finds him hostile and revolting in the end. He treats her "as his prisoner." (377) In Lessing's play *Each His Own Wilderness* Tony, the son, disapproves of all the ideas of his mother and resents her independent activities. He rejects whatever she tries to do for him. She sells the house for his sake, so that he can see the world and broaden his outlook, but he does not like it either. She wants him to live on his own, now that he is twenty-two, so that she can live independently in her own way, but he still demands attention like a child of five and exasperates his mother so much that she has to quit her own house. In her short-story "To Room Nineteen," Susan Rawlings spends her entire life for the children, and finally loses her own life in the process. However, Anna in *The Golden Notebook* finds motherhood quite a soothing and satisfying experience. Her daughter Janet is her "normality." Anna feels: "she anchors me in what is normal in myself." (526) In her moments of turmoil, tension and disintegration, Anna finds comfort and stability in the thoughts of Janet. But then Janet is still a child.

One does not know how she would respond to Anna once Janet starts thinking on her own.

Rose in *Rich Like Us* desperately longs for a child when she first sees Dev, Ram's son from his first wife Mona. She thinks that Mona enjoys the status of the mistress of the house because she has produced a son and performed her role as "a vehicle for the next generation" while she herself "hadn't performed the service for which women are intended." (63-64) Her desire for a son remains unfulfilled and ironically she is got murdered years later at her step-son Dev's behest whose care Mona had made Rose's duty at the time of her own death.

In the game of power within marriage, children who are the blessing of a marriage turn into a device of securing more power over women. Men prefer a large number of children as the "greater the number of pregnancies, the less opportunity women had to compete for power."[55] Children become a device for men to enchain women forcibly in marriage. In an incident in *The Golden Notebook*, the husband, De Silva impregnates his wife against her wishes and then mercilessly abandons her with two kids and no money at Ceylon and comes to live in London. Womaniser as he is, he again pursues women there. Molly and Anna's talk about him is quite revealing:

> He came back. A couple of months ago. He's abandoned his wife, apparently. She's much too good for him, he says, weeping big tears, but not too big, because after all she is stuck with two kids in Ceylon and no money: so he's safe. (69)

Germaine Greer warns woman (in her *The Female Eunuch)* that man may "even determine to impregnate her to break down her self-sufficiency."[56] In *A Proper Marriage*, when Martha is determined to leave Douglas, he threatens her: "I'll give you another baby – that's all; put an end to this nonsense." (351) Aware of the stifling and destructive influence of the unwanted pregnancies, feminists had insisted on, and then succeeded in, getting the abortion legalised so that at least women have control over their bodies. Now, of course, women do not have to submit to the "arbitrariness of conception," but when Lessing wrote these novels woman's biological functions were often exploited by the husbands to keep her enslaved in marriage.

We get a poignant picture in *Rich Like Us* of women suffering because of pregnancies when abortion was not legally allowed. Rose musing on her childhood remembers how, for fear of more children, "loving each other had fallen into disuse" (56) between her parents. Particularly for women, it was tired sex always accompanied with the fear of more mouths to feed. With no provision of legal abortion at that time, "Miscarriages were better than nothing, but in the end you were back to full-term deliveries, your bruised and battered body returned, a loose empty sack to fill up again." (57)

Sahgal's Leela and Lessing's Martha and Alice suffer because abortion was illegal, a crime. Leela in *Storm in Chandigarh* dies during an abortion performed by unskilled hands. After her marriage to Douglas, Martha, in *A Proper Marriage*, is advised by her friends Stella and Alice to see the doctor to know about the methods of birth-control, and warn her that "if you start a baby, then it's illegal not to have it." (25) Martha is appalled to know it and remarks outrageously: "Do you mean to say that a woman's not entitled to decide whether she's going to have a baby or not?" (25)

Martha and Alice both find child-bearing and child-rearing debilitating, frustrating and irritating experiences. Motherhood neither soothes Martha nor brings her closer to her husband as is expected. After the birth of her daughter Caroline, Martha feels as if she has been confined perpetually in the nursing home and calls it a "factory." She hates the business of child-bearing, the cycle of procreation and cries in anguish: "I wish I'd never had a baby at all." (172) Martha's friend Stella experiences similar emotional turmoil after the birth of her baby boy. Both feel as if they are "a couple of cows" and tell their common friend Alice that "we both wish we were dead." (173) Martha repents marrying at a young age and advises her unresponsive infant:

> Two years ago, I was as free as air. I could have done anything, been anything. Because the essence of daydream of every girl who isn't married is just that . . . . Caroline, don't marry young. (228)

Unlike her mother who is always interfering and putting pressures on her, Martha wants her daughter to grow into an independent and free human being. She tells Caroline: "I'll send you to a nursery school, where you are well out of my poisonous influence." (227)

Gradually, Martha too develops tender emotions as a mother and a "desire to hold a small baby in her arms again." She is also aware of the needs of Caroline to have a companion. But she also knows that "if she had another baby, she would be committed to staying here, she would live in the pattern till she dies," that is, to "housekeep and mind babies" (266) which she does not want. And when Douglas insists on having another baby, she feels her "deepest self threatened." (281) Finally, the emotional turmoil is over when maternal emotions of Martha are overpowered by her desire to be free and she decides that she will not go in for another child at all. Her "vision of the brooding mother with the flock of children" and she in their "middle like a queen ant" (304) vanishes as the desire for emancipation become stronger. She rejects her mother's suggestion that she "must sacrifice herself to her children as she had done." (145)

Motherhood is a hindrance in pursuing any career successfully and satisfactorily. Sahgal's Simrit and Lessing's Anna, Molly or Ella try to successfully combine the two equally demanding roles, i.e. motherhood and career. The men all along remain indifferent and selfish and never help women in the process of child-rearing. In the name of mammalian responsibilities, women are condemned to a fettered existence. However, if the child-rearing responsibility is shared by both the parents, the chances of happiness and satisfaction for the family life increase. As Alvin Toffler also observes, "parenting" is a shared responsibility and a shared pleasure."[57] But the responsibility is usually not shared and family proves to be a source of tension for most of the women. This becomes evident from an observation made by Anna in *The Golden Notebook.* During an election campaign, she finds that most of the housewives have no opinion and do only what their husbands say. She attributes woman's lack of will and rationality to family, and comments: "five lonely women going mad quietly by themselves, in spite of husband and children or rather because of them." (174)

Motherhood is considered good only for married women; to be an unwed mother is an offence and her children a stigma or a handicap. In *A Ripple from the Storm*, when Maisie becomes pregnant before her marriage to Binkie, his parents, the Maynards, refuse to accept her and even hesitate to inform Binkie when he is away to war. It is only Andrew, a member of the communist group (to which Martha belongs) who agrees to marry her to give a name to the unborn child. In *The Golden Notebook,* Anna, who has been living with Max Wulf without marriage, marries him when she conceives so that their child (Janet) is not illegitimate. She divorces him after the birth of the daughter.

(vi) Awareness Towards Emancipation

Feminists emphatically insist on the importance of women becoming "aware" of themselves as individuals and shaping their own destinies by assertiveness and self-confidence, and use the term "feminist consciousness" or "consciousness raising" in this context. Juliet Mitchell defines consciousness raising as "the process of transforming the hidden, individual fears of women into a shared awareness of the meaning of them as social problems, the release of anger, anxiety, the struggle of proclaiming the painful and transforming it into the political."[58] While the traditional-minded women accept their "false conditioning" into subordination and dependence without demur, the sensitive and aware women realize the need for individuality and revolt against the established norms by "leaving a marriage that had become an emotional wasteland"[59] for them.

Sahgal's world consists of two types of women characters. The first group consists of women who are happy in the confines of Hindu orthodoxy, and the other of those with a strong sense of individuality and an analytical mind but shuttling between traditional and modern values. In the first group fall women like Lakshmi, Devika and the narrator's mother in *A Time to be Happy,* Mira of *This Time of Morning* and Gauri (apart from her sexual freedom) in *Storm in Chandigarh*. These women are perfectly happy with their position and their roles which they accept ungrudgingly. Mona in *Rich Like Us* and Prabha in *A Time to be Happy* are victims of bigamy, but still they conform to the ideals of subdued womanhood.

In the second group fall Rashmi of *This Time of Morning,* Saroj of *Storm in Chandigarh* and Simrit of *The Day in Shadow*, who are Sahgal's "new women," though the process of awakening in them is quite slow and the revolt comes after much retrospection. However, these thinking and sensitive women have to face a lot of opposition from the narrow-minded and orthodox Indian society, which considers tolerance, patience and forbearance as essential virtues of women. When Rashmi leaves her husband's house, her mother Mira is appalled to know about her separation, for it "was worse than bad news," and was a "moral blow to all she held sacred." (146) Only her father understands her agony and welcomes her decision.

Awareness in a woman that she can live a different but happy and purposeful life is of no avail unless the patriarchal forces in our society support her and do not pressurize her to accept the stereotype as it normally happens. For instance, in a moving story, "Lajwanti," Mulk Raj Anand depicts the helplessness and oppression of a village girl who after the ill-treatment meted out to her by her in-laws comes to live in her father's house. The father, instead, takes her back to them as he is more concerned with the family's "respectability" than the daughter's happiness, who is kicked and tormented even in his presence. The poor woman is "condemned to live"[60] in a real inferno. But Sahgal's women belong to a class where women are still relatively free, and once they decide to break the marriage they do not experience any pressure from their parents to stay married "properly."

However, in Lessing's *A Proper Marriage*, Martha's mother shuts the door and "would not let her in" (377) when Martha, chased by her husband, pleads her mother to give her a shelter for the night. Mrs. Quest has no sympathy with her daughter and declares finally, "go back to him." Martha, however, rejects the stereotype and sets herself free from the social obligation; she leaves her husband and child behind to live a "free," independent life – a life of self-fulfilment. While Sahgal's women take longer to take the bold step to live life in their own way, Lessing's women are bolder and quicker to decide and break the stifling bondage of marriage soon after. However, unlike Martha, Anna and Molly, awareness comes to Marion slowly, and then she also decides to look for freedom and self-esteem in a different way. The awareness of her suppression in marriage makes Marion decide to "live for others" and to do so she takes up "bigger" things in life than "just to please this *creature*," i.e. her husband. The submissive, devoted wife Marion remains all "wrapped up" in him till she gets the revelation that the man she loves is not "anything":

> He's not even very good-looking. He's not even very intelligent – I don't care if he is ever so important and a captain of industry.... My God, for that creature I've ruined my life. (389)

She finally, though quite late, divorces him to fulfil her inner self.

In Lessing's novels, two types of women characters emerge. The first type of women are self-reliant, individual and independent like Martha, Maisie, Anna, Molly, Ella or Julia who repudiate the conventions and seek their own identity and *raison d'etre* in life. The other kind of women, mainly belonging to her older generation, are projected as conventional, conforming to the traditional values, like Mrs. Quest, Mrs. Knowell, Mrs. Maynard or Mrs. Talbot in *A Proper Marriage*. They strongly believe that suffering is a part of a woman's life and have accepted their life in these terms.

The contemporary feminists find segregation or separatism in human relationship inimical for humanity and thus appeal for conformity to the old value of mutuality and "felicity" – the term Marilyn French uses to connote all the qualities that can sweeten life – "for the survival of the institution of marriage."[61] They appeal to men in particular, that they should also involve themselves in marriage and strive for absorbing, fuller and lasting relationship. To reconcile love in marriage needs no *tour de force* but just an inclination on the part of men.

Rashmi in Sahgal's *This Time of Morning* feels "since marriage can be so unhappy, I suppose it can be happy, too, with the right ingredients." (41) The right "ingredients" for a happy marriage are mutuality, communication, honesty and respect for each other. The reason why men outside marriage (like Vishal and Raj) can be caring and understanding is precisely this that their relationship with woman is based on honesty and respect for each other. Discussing Sahgal's works, Jasbir Jain aptly observes: "marriage is neither a system of slavery nor an escape route. It is not even a contract -- for it is wrong to approach it in that spirit. It is a partnership based on respect and consideration and requiring involvement from both."[62] In Lessing's *The Marriage Between Zones Three, Four, and Five* (1980) the marriage between the Queen of Zone Three and the King of Zone Four becomes happy when equality, sweetness and concern replace slavery, brutality and callousness. Lessing's humanist concern is again revealed in her latest novel, *The Fifth Child* (1988), where she advocates the need of fidelity, love, family life and a permanent home, against the noisy background of today's complex world.

Sahgal's marital morality as revealed in her works is based on honesty, mutual trust, consideration, understanding and freedom. She assails selfishness, pretence, self-centredness which result in schism and subsequently in marital breakdown. Traditionally, her women are taught to stay acquiescent, subdued, silent and suffering, but like Saroj, Rashmi or Simrit, they show signs of awakening, reject the stereotype and speak out the truth. They have lived half of their life as submissive and conforming persons; henceforth, they are going to be subversive and "free" beings. The "femininity" is equally imposed upon Lessing's women. There is a constant struggle between the self and the sexist society. Her women do not wish to lose their "self" which has already been damaged in marriage; hence, they defy the institution and break away from their destroyer to seek self-fulfilment.

Sahgal and Lessing do not outrightly repudiate the institution of marriage, but when their women find that they are being oppressed or marginalized, they rebel against the rigid taboos and parochialism of the sexist society. Some of these women remarry or live with men outside marriage because they seek wholeness and complete involvement in relationship. They reject compartmentalization or fragmentation and there is a quest for constructive and meaningful relationship in which the individuals are genuinely and intrinsically interested in each other as people, "not as commodities."[63] They finally emerge as "free-women" looking for a life of self-fulfilment and self-realization.

NOTES

1. Nicholas Abercrombie, Stephen Hill, and Bryan S. Turner, *Dictionary of Sociology* (Harmondsworth: Penguin, 1984), p. 127.
2. Simone de Beauvoir, *The Second Sex*, p. 496.
3. Germaine Greer, *The Female Eunuch*, p. 320.
4. Betty Friedan, *The Second Stage*, p. 36.
5. Lynne Segal, *Is the Future Female ? Troubled Thoughts on Contemporary Feminism*, p. ix.
6. Sheila Rowbotham, *Women, Resistance and Revolution*, p. 2014.
7. J.S. Mill, "The Subjection of Women," *The Feminist Papers*, ed. Alice S. Ross (New York: Bantam, 1974), p. 207.
8. Quoted in Simone de Beauvoir, p. 484.
9. Greer, p. 321.
10. Quoted in Juliet Mitchell, *Woman's Estate* (New York: Vintage, 1973), p. 110.
11. Doris Lessing, *Martha Quest*, p. 156.
12. Doris Lessing, *A Proper Marriage* (1985; rpt. St Albana : Panther, 1977), p. 34.
13. Edmund Spenser, "Epithaiamion," *The New Oxford Book of English Verse 1250-1950*, ed. Helen Gardner (1972; rpt. London: Oxford University Press, 1975), p. 68.
14. Segal, p. 5.
15. Doris Lessing, *A Ripple from the Storm* (1964; rpt. London: Granada, 1981), p. 123.
16. Atma Ram, *Interviews with Indian English Writers* (Calcutta: Writers' Workshop, Greybird, 1983), p. 48.
17. Nayantara Sahgal in a letter to the author, appended at the end.
18. Nayantara Sahgal, *Rich Like Us* (London: Heinemann, 1985), p. 54.
19. Nayantara Sahgal, *The Day in Shadow* (1971; rpt. New Delhi: Bell, 1976), p. 27.
20. Lionel Trilling, *Sincerity and Authenticity* (1971; rpt. Cambridge: Harvard University Press, 1973), p. 124.
21. Nayantara Sahgal, *Storm in Chandigarh*, p. 102.
22. Kate Millett, *Sexual Politics*, p. 33.
23. Gail Putney Fullerton, *Survival in Marriage* (Illinois: Dryden Press Hinsdale, 1977), p. 68.
24. Marilyn French, *Beyond Power: On Women, Men and Morals*, p. 68.

25. Akhileswar Jha, *Modernization and the Hindu Socio-Culture*, p. 97.
26. Shyam Asnani, "New Morality in the Modern Indo-English Novel," *Explorations in Modern Indo-English Fiction*, ed. R.K.Dhawan (New Delhi: Bahri, 1982), p. 68.
27. "Doris Lessing at Stony Brook: An Interview by Jonah Raskin," *A Small Personal Voice: Doris Lessing, Essays, Reviews, Interviews*, ed. Paul Schlueter (New York: Vintage, 1975), p. 71.
28. Doris Lessing, *The Golden Notebook*, p. 24.
29. De Beauvoir, p. 497.
30. Helene Cixous and Catherine Clement, *The Newly Born Woman*, p. 63.
31. Segal, p. 12.
32. De Beauvoir, p. 488.
33. Tim O'Sullivan et. al., *Key Concepts in Communication* (London: Methuen, 1983), p. 42: "There are broadly two types of definitions of communication. The first sees it as a process by which A sends a message to B upon whom it has an effect. The second sees it as a negotiation and exchange of meaning, in which messages, people-in-cultures and 'reality' interact so as to enable meaning to be produced or understanding to occur."
34. Michael Haralambos and Robin Heald, *Sociology: Themes and Perspectives* (Delhi: Oxford University Press, 1980), p. 360.
35. Jasbir Jain, "The Aesthetics of Morality: Sexual Relations in the Novels of Nayantara Sahgal," *The Journal of Indian Writing in English*, 6, No. 1 (Jan. 1978), p. 44.
36. Rollo May, *Power and Innonence: A Search for the Source of Violence* (1972; rpt. London: Fontana Collins, 1976), p. 247.
37. Greer, p. 244.
38. Nayantara Sahgal, *This Time of Morning*, p. 22.
39. Eric Berne, *Sex in Human Loving* (1970; Harmondsworth: Penguin, 1977), p. 125.
40. Nicholas Abercrombie, Stephen Hill and Bryan S. Turner, p. 21: "Anomie" is a "social condition characterized by the breakdown of norms governing social interaction."
41. Nayantara Sahgal writes in response to a letter from the author. See Appendix.
42. De Beauvoir, p. 446.
43. Doris Lessing, *The Grass is Singing*, p. 46.
44. Roberta Rubenstein, *The Novelistic Vision of Doris Lessing: Breaking the Forms of Consciousness*, p. 19.

45. Charles and Liebetrant Sarvan, "D.H. Lawrence and Doris Lessing's *The Grass is Singing,*" *Modern Fiction Studies*, 24, No. 4 (Winter 1978-79), p. 537.
46. De Beauvoir, p. 449.
47. Frederick R. Karl, *A Reader's Guide to the Contemporary English Novel* (London: Thames and Hudson, 1962), p. 282.
48. Berne, p. 123.
49. Nayantara Sahgal, "Adultery in Life and Literature," *The Sunday Standard,* 28 Sept. 1975, p. 6.
50. Betty Friedan, p. 280.
51. Doris Lessing, "Preface," *The Golden Notebook*, p. 10.
52. Mitchell, p. 14.
53. Swami Vivekananda, *The Complete Works of Vivekananda,* Vol. VIII (1847; rpt. Calcutta: Advaita Ashrama, 1971), p. 58.
54. Greer, p. 322.
55. Alvin Toffler, *Previews and Premises* (London: Pan, 1984), p. 127.
56. Greer, p. 244.
57. Toffler, p. 135
58. Mitchell, p. 61.
59. Nayantara Sahgal, "The Virtuous Woman," *The Tribune* (Saturday Plus), Dec. 24, 1988, p. 1.
60. Mulk Raj Anand, *Selected Short Stories,* ed. with an introduction by M.K. Naik (New Delhi: Arnold-Heinemann, 1977), p. 106.
61. French, p. 479.
62. Jasbir Jain, *Nayantara Sahgal* (New Delhi: Arnold-Heinemann, 1978), p. 60.
63. Herman R. Lantz and Eloise C. Snydir, *Marriage: An Examination of the Man Woman Relationship* (New York: John Wiley, 1962), p. VIII. According to them meaningful relationships in marriage "refer to relationships in which the individuals are intrinsically interested in each other as people, not as commodities, and in which each person has the opportunity to grow intellecutally and emotionally.

Free Woman ?

> You think . . . that divorce will be the end of something that has become intolerable. What you don't know is that you are getting into another way of life that can be just as painful, that divorce is only the beginning. (A lonely divorcee, quoted in Gail Putney Fullerton's *Survival in Marriage*)

For centuries marriage was considered to be the destiny for woman irrespective of the fact whether she was happily married or was miserable due to constant oppression by man in the patriarchal set-up. However, a possibility of freedom from endless suffering in unhappy marriage appeared with divorce, separation or annulment of marriage under law. Divorce is a process of giving legal recognition to the breaking up of a relationship already shattered by irreconcilable disparity in the character of two persons or by broken faith, and bitter tensions. For ensuring harmony in the marital relations, an acceptance and adjustment of the wishes, attitudes and sentiments of both the partners is necessary. But when the needs, wishes or individuality of one of the partners is ignored then this results in discord. "Divorce," as Marilyn French says, "like marriage, is morally neutral, it is good; insofar as it ends a long-term intimacy, it is to be lamented."[1] But certainly divorce gives freedom to women to get rid of an existence of suffering due to male-aggression or gender oppression.

In India, traditionally, the matrimonial ties are considered irrevocable. The "Hindu Dharma" expects from a wife complete obedience and devotion to her husband. She is expected to completely merge her ego with her husband's, and to strictly follow the ideal of *Pativrata*:

> As river merging itself in the ocean loses its identity, so a wife was supposed to merge her individuality with that of her husband. Her only concern in life was to see that all services needed by her husband were properly performed by her, the satisfaction of her husband being her sole joy in life . . . there was no question of raising a word against him even when he was found to be ill-tempered, vicious, diseased or a drunkard.[2]

In India, the blessing for the married woman is always "Sada Suhagan Raho" (i.e. May you never lose your husband). To have a husband was the greatest blessing for a woman even if he was evil because society recognized woman only through husband. A single woman had no status in society. Hence, there were practices like "Sati" (Self-immolation of widows on the pyre of the deceased husband) because a woman's existence without a husband was thought to be meaningless. While some performed Sati willingly, knowing the plight of widows in Hindu society, others were forced to die on the husband's pyre. We get in Sahgal's *Rich Like Us* ghastly accounts of the way widows were forced to perform Sati, "a revolting system of suicide and murder."[3] Sonali, reading her grandfather's manuscript written in 1915, finds how if a widow could not bear the flames and tried to get out of the pyre her relatives would thrust her back into the fire and beat her with logs of wood so that she fell unconscious and did not try to run out of the fire again. (123-25) Sonali's grandfather's father who was a crusader against Sati was very happy when in 1829 the horrid rule of Sati was abolished. However, when he died, a couple of days later his wife who herself was a non-believer in Sati was forcibly taken to a pyre next to her husband's and most cruelly burnt to death by her relatives in the absence of her nineteen-year-old son. (134) Even today some stray cases of Sati (like Roop Kanwar's performing Sati in 1987) take place but now the furore against such practices is great. In this kind of set-up, the question of divorce or separation for a married Indian woman did not arise. Hence, for centuries there was no provision for a legal divorce. A woman could not remarry even after the death of her husband, though a man could abandon his wife and remarry any time.

The concept of marriage as a sacrament and an indissoluble union was pervasive in the West also for centuries, and divorce was only a male's privilege. Woman was seen only in relation to man. She had no life of her own. As Gilbert and Gubar comment in *The Madwoman in the Attic*, to be selfless is not only to be noble, it is to be dead. But the woman who refuses to be selfless and acts on her own initiative irritates the society and is unwelcome. In the western societies, there were no grounds for which a woman could divorce her husband until Roman women gained the right to divorce in the days of the Empire. However, Protestants took a somewhat more liberal stand on the question of divorce. "Luther seems to have believed that only adultery and desertion were adequate grounds for divorce. . . . However, in addition to adultery and desertion, cruelty and 'refusal to conjugal duty' (which meant refusal of sexual intercourse) were also considered grounds for divorce by most Protestant churches."[4] John Milton wrote a series of pamphlets in favour of divorce in the years between 1643 and 1645 but it was only in 1857 that judicial divorce (divorce granted by a court of law) became available in England. And it was only in 1968 that the divorce laws were made more liberal.

The liberalization of divorce has come as a great help to save women from endless oppression, or torture in marriage. And now apart from the usual grounds of adultery, cruelty, greed etc., divorce can be granted on the mutual-consent basis, if both the partners agree and are bent upon final separation; in America this is known as "no-fault" divorce.

Both Sahgal and Lessing show women suffering in marriage and then deciding to come out of the stifling bondage by opting for divorce. They are not concerned with the legal aspects of the divorce, viz., the delays in legal process or rigorous legal clauses which make divorce difficult for women, but are rather concerned with the repercussions of divorce on women. Both depict their women deciding to opt for divorce rather than live a suffocating life of injustice and agony. Saroj, Simrit, Rashmi, Martha, Molly and Anna all leave their husbands or break the marriage which does not allow them to be free and to live life in their own way. Both Lessing and Sahgai depict that though divorce frees them from the agony and suffering of an unhappy or unjust relationship still it does not solve the problems and women have to continue to struggle and suffer on various levels – economic, emotional and psychological. As such the questions arise: does a sexist society easily accept a woman's freedom? Does a woman find real happiness in her new role as divorce? Does she really become free after divorce? These and some other related issues have been explored in the selected novels of Lessing and Sahgal.

Divorce which is admittedly a relief from the painful life of a wrong marriage, is hardly enough to re-establish the woman socially, psychologically or financially. Even after divorce, the aggrieved or relieved woman does not find herself in the same situation as before marriage. Despite the wounds inflicted in the unsuccessful marriage which have to be borne for a long time, a woman has to further bear the onslaughts of a harsh society which does not allow her to be free and happy. Divorce is the beginning of another phase of troubles.

In the past the role of the divorced woman was to withdraw from the society and hide her shame. The divorcee was shunned by friends, and spoken of in hushed whispers by her relatives. The divorcee was not sure whether she was expected to grieve or to celebrate, to feel ashamed or relieved. The Indian society still does not consider divorce to be something good or healthy despite the liberal divorce laws. As Rama Mehta puts it, "the position of the divorced or separated woman . . . (has) only marginally improved for the upper middle class."[5] Divorce in Indian society in general is considered a social stigma and a big scandal for a woman who is treated as if she is accursed with some disease. Probably, this makes most of the oppressed women dare not break their unhappy marriage and silently accept physical and mental torture instead. However, the trends have changed in recent times. Instead of clinging to a sterile and oppressive relationship, more and more women are asserting themselves and are seeking freedom by way of divorce, even if they have to incur wrath of society or their family. Rashmi in *This Time of Morning* annoys her mother who does not talk to her when she learns of Rashmi's decision of separation. Rashmi's mother belongs to the generation where women are judged by endurance, submission and devotion to whatever fate provides them in the form of husband and his family. She firmly believes that "endurance was a test of character"[6] which her daughter could not qualify. The title of the novel itself is quite symbolic: on the one hand, the nation, the mother figure comes out of darkness of colonialism, and on the other Rashmi and other women in the novel gradually come out of the narrow, dark, slavish, patriarchal bonds, answering the call of their own individuality.

Sahgal's women, e.g. Rashmi, Saroj, Simrit quite often feel smothered in marriage and miss the elements of *eros*, *philos* and *agape* (the terms used by Greeks for desire, friendship and affection respectively) in their relationship. Divorce is an expression of their dissatisfaction over their stale and sterile marital relationship. It also expresses their desire to live a life of intense, absorbing and more congenial relationship. Saroj in *Storm in Chandigarh* longs for friendship, tenderness and frankness from Inder, but since her jealous, unreasonable husband never bothers to understand her needs, she decides to walk out of her rotten, conventional confinement, with all the children to live a life of her own. But while *Storm in Chandigarh* focuses mainly on Saroj's unhappy experience within married life and we do not know what her life is going to be after she leaves her husband, in another novel the focus is entirely on a woman's life after divorce.

Sahgal's very closely autobiographical novel *The Day in Shadow* narrates the experience of Simrit who has, like Saroj, after many years of married life decided to put an end to her unhappy marriage. Through Simrit, Sahgal expounds various aspects of divorce and its implications for a lonely woman. Simrit's decision of divorce lands her into multifarious problems. In the traditional society, where a married woman is respected more than a single woman, a divorcee is more or less ostracized or shunned as if she were a pollution. The husband's social status or official position becomes a touchstone through which the worth of a woman is measured. After her divorce, Simrit soon realizes that it is basically a "husband-centred world"[7] where a free woman has no place; her individual contribution and social standing are meaningless in this male-oriented society. Like Sahgal, Simrit is a journalist and a more well-known writer but finds that people are more interested in her husband and often ask her "what does your husband do?" (6) Instead of showing concern for the agonized lonely woman, they add fuel to the fire by insisting on the "husband" and his status, etc. Simrit reflects on the whole graceless affair: "Wasn't it odd, when you were standing there yourself, fully a person, not to be asked what you did?" (6) Shortly after her divorce, in a posh party being attended by top bureaucrats of the Ministry of Petroleum and aristocrats and debonairs of Delhi's upper strata, people are surprised to find her alone. One of the organizers of the party "was studying her solicitously, as if divorce were a disease that left pock marks." (4) Simrit is a woman with a strong sense of individuality and had "never accepted a world where men did things and women waited for them." (6) Her independent, bold, self-reliant attitude separates her from the traditional women who religiously follow the foot-steps of their husband and worship him like a god. Simrit is surprised to find that people around her mourn the divorce and hesitate to accept it as soothing and life-giving at least to the person who had suffered prolonged suppression and domination. When Som's company lawyer Moolchand visits her, he begins his conversation condoling, "as if someone had died" : "I want to tell you how sad I consider all this . . . so unbelievable . . . all my sympathies . . . the children . . . anything I can do." (54) The Managing Director of Oil Products Ltd., Mr. Shah, whom Simrit meets to seek his advice on the consent terms, also does not consider divorce to be something positive as he believes that "divorce is not part of our tradition." (146) Sadly, no one tries to look into the reason of divorce. Divorce, when it comes to Simrit, is not easy either:

> It was painful how the connection continued, like a detached heartbeat. The tissue of a marriage could be dissolved by human acts, but its anatomy went on and on. And skeletons could endure for a million years. Just living together, daily routine produced that uncanny durability. It made the question of whether one had loved or not, been loved or not, been the transgressor or transgressed against, trivial by comparison. (64)

Even after divorce the woman often experiences a sense of inability to control or mould her life. In *The Day in Shadow*, Sahgal reveals the psychological, financial and other existential problems which a woman has to face as part of her punishment for leaving her husband. After divorce while a man feels free from all moral, social and financial responsibilities, a woman feels as if her inner self "has gone to pieces" (51) or like "a person thrown out of a train in the night and forced to find his way home in the dark." (51-52) Gail Putney Fullerton remarks that the final separation is bewildering: "It is like pushing against a door that suddenly gives way."[8] Even after divorce or separation which a woman mainly seeks for her peace, freedom and independence, she finds herself in troubled waters again. The male jealousy and cruelty operate even after divorce.

Doris Lessing uses the phrase "pattern of behaviour" in *A Proper Marriage* to indicate man's jealous response to wife's decision of divorce. Towards the end of this novel, when Martha overcomes her initial reluctance to leave Douglas and her decision becomes publicly known, several women of the town come to her to congratulate her on what they could not do in their own lives. They also blurt out the truth of their unhappy marital relationship. But her husband gets desperate and tries everything from threats and appeals to stop her from leaving him. Lessing gives a psychologically realistic description of the behaviour in which a man indulges when he learns that his wife is going to desert him:

> When a woman left her husband, or threatened to leave him – that is, a woman of her type, who insisted on her rights to behave as a man would – then the husband went through certain actions like an automaton, beginning with confiscating the contraceptives, threatening to make her forcibly pregnant, accusing her of multifarious infidelities, and ending in self-abasing weeping appeals that she should change her mind and stay . . . they were involved in a pattern of behaviour which they could not alter.[9]

Douglas tries his best to stop Martha and threatens to impregnate her in order to break her self-sufficiency. He even indulges in physical abuse to terrorize her, but nothing could alter Martha's rock-hard decision to break the stale, unjust, one-sided relationship. And when Martha finally leaves him, he spies on her in order to blackmail her and win public sympathy. His jealousy comes down to the level of meanness and he demands back the money she spent on her personal items like "sandals" or "sweater" when she was staying with him:

> He informed her that in the year before she had left him, she had bought goods to the value of $ 20 at the shops, and he was incurring a great deal of extra expense due to her having left him. . . . He produced an account like a shopkeeper's on a sheet of stiff paper: Item one pair of shoes; Item one sweater, 25 s.; and so on, handing it to her with a sentimental and appealing smile.[10]

Even when the woman is not the one asking for divorce, she still has to bear with such pettiness in her husband. In *The Golden Notebook* when Richard is contemplating a divorce from Marion to marry his young secretary, he delimits his wife's monthly expenditure and checks her accounts regularly; Marion unveils his meanness to Anna:

> Would you believe it, that he could be so mean? He's as rich as hell. Do you know, we are among the one per cent of people as rich as – but he examines my accounts every month. He boasted that we were among the top one per cent, but I bought a model dress and he complained.[11]

Sahgal in *The Day in Shadow* also reveals the ubiquitous "pattern of behaviour." Som Raman, a business magnate, agrees to divorce his wife for ultimate commercial benefits. Also, in order to take revenge on his wife Simrit, he imposes cruel divorce terms on her in a satanically shrewd way. Simrit out of ignorance and good faith signs the consent terms without really reading them. Simrit's efforts to get rid of these unfair, unjudicious terms – "the document [that] trapped and maimed her" (39) – mutually and amicably, fail. Simrit is a woman who is "bleeding to death with taxes." (146) She has been "used as convenience." (168) Even after divorce her husband, in order to save his own income tax, thrust cruel consent terms on her according to which she has to pay "huge taxes" (55) on the shares worth six lacs, which are presently in her name but will go to her son Brij, aged sixteen, after nine years, i.e. when he attains the age of twenty-five. Simrit pleads with Som's lawyer: "I don't want the shares left in my name. As long as they are, I'II have to pay this crippling tax and whatever I earn will just be wiped out by the tax. " (56) The answer in response to her request overtly reveals the narrow, money-minded male attitude: "Because, Mrs. Raman, there would be a big gifts tax if we made a trust." (56) The lawyer believes that these terms are quite reasonable and were drawn with the consent of both the parties: "I must remind you, Mrs. Raman," Moolchand continues in the same formal vein, "that this was negotiated settlement to which you gave your consent." (60) Simrit meets Som to appeal to his conscience and to find some way out but he proposes a fresh agreement, which is more cruel than the previous one. Simrit is horrified to hear his irresponsible suggestion:

> What we can do is make a new agreement. Let's say you can use the income from those shares—if you don't marry—and until they're transferred to the children. Of course I'd have to stop the support you're getting now. And you'd have to pay the taxes on the Corpus, but since you'd be using the income that would be quite fair. (221)

Simrit rejects the fresh terms outright and thus the problem remains unresolved. Raj also could not understand the motive behind such an agreement:

> "Whatever made Som stick a document like that on you? Revenge for what?"
> Simrit frowned. "It wasn't revenge. It was just Som."
> "Just Som is what I've been trying to get at," said Raj. "What was Som like?"
> "Well he liked to have the last word. The terms were his parting shot, like his not sending the car for Merriwether." (225)

Simrit continues to be in a state of agony till Raj angelically emerges to protect her and later marries her. While Som belongs to the artificial and material world of rat race, Raj's world is different. Opposed to the attitude of banal calculations is the spirit of humanism that Raj, a Christian, embodies in his relationship with Simrit. Simrit does not leave Som for Raj's sake; she only shares his friendliness and tenderness though later both are tied in matrimonial knot. While Som never tried to fathom her depth, with Raj she has a more satisfying and absorbing relationship. Raj not only shakes her benumbed mind to awakening but makes her shed her shadows and live as a bold, assertive woman. But ironically, somewhere deep down, the patriarchal attitudes are embedded in Raj too. Raj very suddenly announces his marriage to Simrit before his elderly friend Ram Krishan, without even consulting her and giving her time to think over. Simrit is surprised at the abrupt announcement, but then accepts it silently. (231-32)

Sahgal here effectively reveals the predicament of a woman after divorce. She purposely chooses an intelligent, sensitive and aware woman, who is a writer and a free lance journalist, but who is very shrewdly trapped in a brutal divorce settlement, to show that a woman can be easily used by a man for his convenience. In her essay "Of Divorce and Hindu Woman," Sahgal writes:

> I wanted to show how even in a free country like ours where women are equal citizens, a woman can be criminally exploited without its creating a ripple. Again, I am not speaking of any recognizable form of exploitation against which most people will naturally raise a cry. If a man beats his wife, for instance, hardly anyone will condone the fact. But if at divorce he inflicts a financial settlement on her that enslaves her with taxes and makes it impossible for her to make a decent living, no one will take any notice because this is a kind of beating where blood and bruises don't show. But in addition, and this is the crux of the matter – nobody bothers about it even when they do. Simrit in this story finds she has to serve as a tax convenience for her ex-husband all her life, and that tied up in this way, she will never be able to make an adequate living for herself.[12]

As A.V. Krishna Rao comments while discussing Sahgal's *The Day in Shadow*, "Mrs. Sahgal's fictional probe into the cancerous proliferation of social hypocrisy and political pretence in modern India is incisive like that of a surgeon's knife but is tempered with compassion and love. Its analysis and interpretation of the human predicament is informed of newer and truer insights into the human psyche."[13] Through Simrit's divorce, Sahgal thus makes a strong plea for a change and revitalization of the Indian society.

While woman often finds herself in trouble due to financial pressures, man's condition improves substantially after divorce; he becomes richer with practically no burden and responsibility on him. Overburdened with the responsibility of children and home, with no independent income of her own in most cases, a woman has to depend on the little alimony which the court of law grants in her favour as part of divorce settlement. Since the judges and the law-makers are men, so the law also works in the interest of men, and the woman who has to bring up children, usually gets no help from the father of children. In the case of a working woman, usually alimony is not granted on the grounds that she is earning on her own. But a woman's job is less paying than a man's because in the interest of family she cannot pursue a career and often takes up part-time or less demanding, and hence less paying, jobs. As a result even though they are working, after divorce women find their financial position not very sound. After divorce, as Marilyn French puts it: "in an overwhelming number of cases . . . men become singles and women become single mothers. Women's incomes decline by 73 per cent in the first year after divorce; men's incomes *increase* by 42 per cent. The father is better off: the children are often hungry."[14] Germaine Greer also observes that the easy divorce laws have increased the financial insecurity of women. She writes:

> women are not signed up for life in the marriage contract because divorce is always possible, but as it stands, divorce works in the male interests, not only because it was designed and instituted by man, but because divorce still depends on money and independent income. Married women seldom have either.[15]

No doubt, women do "two-thirds of the world's work, provide 45 per cent of its food, earn 10 per cent of its income, and own 1 per cent of its property."[16] A woman, thus, even in purely economic terms suffers greatly in the world of male supremacy. And sometimes the fear of economic hardship alone may hold woman back in unhappy marriages.

In *The Day in Shadow,* Simrit who writes only occasional articles in newspapers has no regular income of her own. Besides, she has to pay income tax on the shares, which her husband has kept in her name to save his own income tax. Simrit, with her son Brij and an unspecified number of daughters, struggles hard to maintain a rented flat which is "too expensive for her." (33) There are no basic amenities like a regular supply of milk or a phone connection. However, she tries to overcome her problems with her characteristic "toughness of undivided integrity." (38)

In Lessing's works, though women are not financially exploited as in Sahgal's *The Day in Shadow*, yet they also do not get any financial help from the husbands whose children they have to bring up on their own. Anna Wulf in *The Golden Notebook* lives on the royalty she gets from her successful novel, *Frontier of War*. Molly also receives no financial aid from her immensely wealthy ex-husband Richard and, hence, works in a theatre for her and their son Tommy's survival. Like marriage, divorce is also tied to responsibility. Man, however, detaches himself from all kinds of responsibilities, moral or financial, the moment separation takes place. Indeed, the "old advice about how to keep a woman quiet and submissive – keep her barefoot in winter and pregnant in summer – has been adapted to the twentieth-century industrial capitalistic world – keep her poor."[17]

Even on the emotional level, divorce does not bring easy happiness or freedom to women. It turns out to be a traumatic experience, a shock and often disintegrates a poised and amiable woman's balanced personality and disturbs her psyche. In fact, to free oneself from the past, and to soothe the wounds of a broken marriage, one needs moral strength and time which ultimately prove to be the healing factors. The social responses also add to the sense of trauma, since a divorced woman is seen as a culprit or as a pitiable creature which increases the sense of deprivation, loneliness and insecurity.

In *The Day in Shadow*, after divorce Simrit feels tormented as if she is suppressed under the "emotional debris" (16) of the shattered relationship. Sometimes she is filled with "unreasoning dread, as if an assassin waited there in the dark for her." (16) After she comes out of the party, when Raj asks her if she enjoyed it, Simrit remarks:

> "How can I enjoy anything? I can't even begin to think straight till things are settled at the flat." She had moved in so recently, it was not yet home. "I feel so disorganized." (14)

Referring to the divorced Indian woman, Tara Ali Baig comments: "life for the woman who has been deserted or divorced is far more grim. . . . In many cases they have problems, however, for this is a society that seems to resent the single woman."[18] Thus, to get freedom as a woman in a man's world and the desire to commit oneself to some lasting satisfying *rasion d'etre* remains largely unfulfilled. A free woman experiences not only an awful feeling of disgust, loneliness and futility but she longs for companionship and togetherness more desperately than before. In the beginning of *The Golden Notebook*, Lessing's "Free Women," Anna and Molly, are able to live "free" of men and marriage, are engaged in a what's wrong-with-men-and-marriage session. Their discussion vividly reveals the precariousness of their freedom. Anna and Molly develop a number of affairs after divorce in search of companionship and permanence in life but are repeatedly disappointed and deserted by men who come to them for their sexual gratification only. While Molly finally decides to remarry, Anna feels so desperately alone that she cannot sleep without a man. Paul Schlueter rightly remarks: "Probably more than in any other novel, *The Golden Notebook* captures the authentic quality of what it is to be a woman, especially a woman in a man's world, and even more especially a woman who frankly admits the existence of her sexuality, her neuroses, her intellect, her desperation in living, her disgust at the mediocre so feverishly sought by those of either sex who are themselves mediocre, her refusal to compromise her essential being."[19] Lessing's Anna and Molly are quite resilient and have the capability to "create order, to create a new way of looking at life," (80) but even they feel broken, forlorn, forsaken, "insecure" and "uprooted." (31) Anna, no doubt, enjoys a certain amount of physical and financial free lom; however, she too has been "afflicted with an awful feeling of disgust, of futility" (58) and insecurity. When a sick ugly man follows her off the underground, grinning triumphantly at her retreat from his lewd urges, she again feels panic, and as if to regain her balance and to calm herself, she buys fruits at a stand, smells the tart clean smell, touches the smooth or faintly hairy skins. (382-83) Though she writes fiction and does party work as a dedicated Communist, yet there is an "emotional vacuum" in her life. As she writes in her diary, she has joined the Communist Party out of a "need for wholeness, for an end to the split, divided, unsatisfactory way we all live." (171) She is still dependent on men for "having sex, for 'being serviced,' for 'being satisfied'" (44) but she is at least free enough to have a number of short affairs.

However, even this free existence is no promise of constant happiness. When Michael after four years of togetherness leaves Anna, there is a disintegration of her being. She feels as if everything is "divided off and split up." (273) When Michael rings Anna for the last time to inform her that he will not come, she feels as if:

> an awful black whirling chaos is just inside me, waiting to move into me. I must go to sleep quickly, before I become that chaos, I am trembling with misery and with tiredness.... Tomorrow, I think – tomorrow – I 'II be responsible, face my future, and refuse to be miserable. Then I sleep, but before I am even asleep I can hear myself crying, the sleep-crying this time all pain, no enjoyment in it all. (360)

After having a happy life full of love, the blow of separation becomes more severe and painful for woman. When Anna's alter ego, Ella, is deserted by her lover Paul, she too feels cracked up, as if she is "in pieces." (311) In fact, her whole "life was shaped around a man who would not return to her." (305) Paul's presence and his demanding and possessive nature had so conditioned Ella that even after Paul "had left her . . . everything she did, said or felt, still referred to him." She is utterly miserable when Paul plays a fraud: "She was listless and flat. It was as if Paul had taken with him, not only all her capacity for joy, but also her will." (305) She loses her will to enjoy the things, the places, the emotions, the happiness, which she earlier shared with Paul; as she says: "the truth is that my happiness with Paul was more important to me than anything and where has that landed me? Alone, frightened to be alone." (312) There is a total disintegration of her personality and the "emotional vacuum" (313) in fact deepens. In their new-found freedom, problems still exist and disappointments in getting love continue.

Men also need women as women need men but they can break a relationship at will, and while they have a secure family life with wives at home, women rest their whole happiness in a man and hence, his desertion leaves them lonelier and broken, disintegrating. Women in this world of male supremacy can depend for comfort and understanding, for solace and company on other women like them.

The process of women developing solidarity among themselves is defined as "sisterhood," when women cease to be rivals of each other or stop competing for the attention of a male, and develop deep "social relationship with one another."[20] Feminists exhort women that they should protect, advise and boost each other's morale to face the male-hegemony. As G. Alison Raymond also tells women, if they "do not take initiative to change conditions no one else is likely to do so."[21] Sisterhood aims at cutting across the racial, political, class or age barriers.

Freud detected jealousy as a feminine trait, but neither in Sahgal nor in Lessing women manifest it. On the contrary, they bolster up each other, offer solace to, and help and support each other. The chief aim of sisterhood is to help women in distress irrespective of colour and class. Feminists repeatedly warn women: "None of us can be free until all are free."[22]

In Lessing's works, sisterhood largely exists among the white women. Lessing's heroines are quite removed from the problems of black women. When sometimes they are ready to do something good for them, the black women remain aloof from the developmental activities, probably because their men do not want them to be educated and aware. Hence, the black women suffer from double tyranny – from the male supremacy and from the racists. In *A Ripple from the Storm* Martha as a communist welfare worker visits the location to give a lecture on personal hygiene, viz., "How to Keep Your Body Clean," "How to Feed Your Family," etc. To her surprise no black woman turns up in the meeting. (199) In *A Ripple from the Storm*, the solidarity among the white women is invigoratingly highlighted by Lessing. Martha is helped by the kind, benevolent comrade Jasmine, whenever she is in trouble financially or emotionally. Martha also helps Maisie when the latter is in the family way and successfully arranges her marriage with Andrew. Again Martha in *The Four Gated City* helps Lynda to be rehabilitated to some extent.

The best example of sisterhood can be seen in *The Golden Notebook*. Anna and Molly, separated from their husbands, live together, provide security, support and company to each other without encroaching on each other's privacy or identity. Sisterhood is not binding on them. Anna, when she likes, moves out to a separate flat without ill feeling for Molly. Men accuse women who live together of being lesbians. Ella protests against the false allegation:

> Paul dislikes Ella's relationship with Julia. He sees it as a pact against him, and makes professional jokes about the lesbian aspects of this friendship. At which Ella says that in that case, his friendships with men are homosexual? (214)

Lessing's women are not separatists. They seek wholeness in a male world itself. Though jealousy has been alleged to be a feminine trait, there is no jealousy between Molly and Marion, Richard's second wife . Molly even infuses necessary courage in Marion to assert her individuality against the raucous, hostile and oppressive attitude of Richard. Lessing's women help each other, confide in each other and whatever freedom is possible it comes with the help of the women friends alone.

In contrast with Lessing's women who are more strong and Amazonian and like Nora help themselves to evade imposition of the male hegemony, Sahgal's women depend on some help to escape oppression and exploitation which in their cases is usually provided by a man – a friend or a father who often helps them to come out of the miserable relationship, or gives them moral strength to smash the taboos and assert their identity to live a meaningful life. In India still the number of "free" women financially independent and willing to take a drastic decision is quite limited and often in the novels of the early 70s women look towards men for emancipation and help. Vishal in *Storm in Chandigarh*, Raj in *The Day in Shadow* and Rakesh in *This Time of Morning* are instrumental in giving new directions to Saroj, Simrit and Rashmi respectively, showing them the way to live life meaningfully. Apart from being down-to-earth, practical and understanding human beings, they have the extraordinary "capacity to counsel patience."[23] As one critic observes, these "men are strikingly similar – intelligent, articulate, compassionate, committed to preserving the values of justice and moderation."[24]

While Vishal in *Storm in Chandigarh* awakens Saroj's sensibility and prepares her to leave her jealous, unreasonable husband, it is in fact Gauri, her cousin, who gives her shelter in the end. Sisterhood is more pronounced in Sahgal's *Rich Like Us*, where Sonali, a spinster and an I.A.S officer, extends all help to Ram's second wife Rose against the oppression of her stepson Dev who intends to usurp her assets and wealth by forging cheques. Sonali consults a top lawyer to help the poor, unwanted English lady. She even seeks the help of an influential bureaucrat, her colleague Ravi Kachru, in the matter. Sonali often takes Rose out for lunch and to cinema to lessen her loneliness. Despite her concern and help Rose, however, is murdered by Dev's men in the end.

Rose once saves Mona from burning when the latter tries to commit suicide, unable to bear the agony any more which started after Ram brought Rose as the second wife.[25] After this incident, Mona who earlier never accepted the "intruder" in her life, now welcomes her with open arms as her sister – "We are sisters!" (139) She develops a deep relationship with her and often asks her about Rose's parents in London. (141) She starts seeking Rose's help and advice in the household matters. When she is dying, she is unmindful of Ram's assurances, and looks for Rose for comfort who is holding her hand fast in her own. Mona extracts a promise from Rose that she (Rose) will look after Dev and his newly-married wife and treat them as her own; "She was looking at Rose. 'She's yours now.' And Rose stepped into the shoes Mona had vacated, a desolate place she no longer wanted for herself." (166) Thus, Sahgal's women, in her later novels in particular, do help and provide comfort to each other whenever necessary.

Lessing's women are "boulder-pushers" (*The Golden Notebook*, 215); they are seekers of truth and fight against cruelty, slavery, and violence to build a balanced and nobler world "full of people who don't hate and fear and murder." (*The Golden Notebook*, 604) Her "free woman" is far from contented and happy, but she chooses an independent way of life because it is less miserable than that of conventional married woman. Even though freedom gives her some happiness and independence to be one's original self, as Marion says, to "live as you like . . . Do as you like," (275) yet the suffering persists. A free woman is exposed to dangers at every level and has to pay a heavy price in terms of her exploitation and harassment. In the West, "Free Women" are usually taken as sex-hungry and men find them "much more exciting than the dull tied women," (*The Golden Notebook*, 441) and are eager to have sex with them especially when their wives are away; as Anna puts it:

> Now we *free women* know that the moment the wives of our men friends go into the nursing home, dear Tom, Dick and Harry come straight over, they always want to sleep with one of their wives' friends. God knows why, a fascinating psychological fact among so many, but it's a fact. (47)

And as Molly Hite comments while discussing Lessing's works, "paradoxically, a free woman is one who is available to men, whether or not she wants to play the roles of mistress, comforter, and therapist that they require of her."[26]

In India also an unmarried, divorced or separated woman is equally exposed to dangers. She is often "used as convenience," and is sexually harassed, physically exploited and morally demoralized. Sahgal gives a glimpse of this through Pixie and Sumer Singh's affair in *The Day in Shadow*. Sumer Singh, a sex-hungry Minister, misuses an independent girl Pixie for the few kind things he has done for her, like giving her a "place to live in and a job." (188) But when she refuses to please him, he threatens her with dire consequences and tells her: "You're nothing but a cheap stray." (193) Sahgal's Devi in *A Situation in New Delhi* and Sonali in *Rich Like Us* are more free and independent than her earlier women. However, they too are intimidated by men. Sonali is pressurized to work in accordance with the wishes of senior officers and Ministers. She, however, retains her assertiveness and dignity and refuses to be their puppet and resigns the job instead. This is the price she has to pay for maintaining her freedom. It is only Devi among Sahgal's women who is not exposed to any dangers and enjoys some freedom like the women in the West who can have a number of affairs with men. While a married life cannot be blended with or remains incompatible with freedom or career for the women, a free woman is also unfulfilled and is considered merely as an easy catch.

Fear of loneliness, insecurity, emotional vacuum, financial pressures and unjust division of responsibility make the divorcees "realise better than the single persons that married life, at large, is satisfying, and this consciousness makes them plan to return to it by remarriage."[27] Remarriage or settling down again in marriage is not anti-feminist, it rather amounts to maturity and better understanding of the ideals of marriage which insists on "life-long 'till death do us part' commitment arising from mutual love and selflessness."[28] They return to marriage in the hope of "co-existence,"[29] in the hope of a world "shared" equally by both the sexes. In the West one in every three marriages ends in break-up and divorce is spreading like an epidemic. Hence, countries like Britain are seriously considering tightening the divorce law, e.g. by banning divorce at least within three years of marriage. Thus, in Europe the stability of marriage and family is being re-stressed. Remarriage also amounts to transcending the trivial self-created sexual prejudices and reaching out for the world where the male and the female have relations based on equality and understanding. Remarriage, however, can be helpful only if husbands are ready to care and share; otherwise the ordeals of the woman in the patriarchal set-up will continue.

Despite the fact that in India remarriage is not very popular, Simrit in *The Day in Shadow* remarries as she can resume her life anew with Raj. The practice of remarriage is more prevalent in the West where "women feel more uncomfortable about answering 'divorced' to questions of marital status than about answering 'housewife' to questions of occupational status. . . . For whatever combination of reasons, divorced women have the highest marriage rate of any group of women in the United States."[30]

The knowledge of their dependence on men makes Anna cry in *The Golden Notebook*: "'I'm not free,' said Anna. . . . 'Marion, I'd like to be married. I don't like living like this.'" (277) After remaining a free woman for long, Molly too finally decides to remarry. (636) The reward of freedom is, thus, insecurity and loneliness. If love within marriage is not possible, it is further difficult after divorce. Like Lessing and Sahgal, many contemporary women writers such as Anita Brookner, Eva Figes and Emma Tennant explore the theme of freedom and loneliness of free women in their works.

Sahgal and Lessing, the iconoclasts, trenchantly bring out that even after achieving cherished freedom in all spheres, women are not truly free and happy as they envisage, and have to pay a heavy price for their independence. A free woman feels lonelier and unprotected in a sexist society which is ready to crush her identity and individuality at every opportunity. The realization thus dawns on her that while divorce provides one kind of freedom, i.e. freedom from oppression and exploitation by the husband, it creates new forms of sufferings and problems as well. Most of Sahgal's and Lessing's women remarry not because they are anti-feminists nor because they are willing to return to oppression within marriage; on the contrary they envision an organized whole world there, as Cynthia Cockburn puts it, "the good qualities deemed masculine – courage, strength and skill, for instance – and the good qualities seen as feminine – tenderness, the ability to feel and express feelings – should be the qualities available to all."[31]

NOTES

1. Marilyn French, *Beyond Power: On Women, Men and Morals*, p. 504.
2. Quoted in Promila Kapur, *Marriage and the Working Women in India* (Delhi: Vikas, 1970), p. 9.
3. Nayantara Sahgal, *Rich Like Us*, p. 121.
4. Gail Putney Fullerton, *Survival in Marriage*, p. 395.
5. Rama Mehta, *Divorced Hindu Woman* (Delhi: Vikas, 1975), p. 168.
6. Nayantara Sahgal, *This Time of Morning*, p. 147.
7. Nayantara Sahgal, *The Day in Shadow*, p. 2

8. Fullerton, p. 446.
9. Doris Lessing, *A Proper Marriage*, pp. 368-69.
10. Doris Lessing, *A Ripple from the Storm* , p. 30.
11. Doris Lessing, *The Golden Notebook*, p. 277.
12. Nayantara Sahgal, "Of Divorce and Hindu Woman," *The Hindustan Times*, 18 December 1971, p. 7.
13. A.V. Krishna Rao, *Nayantara Sahgal: A Study of her Fiction and Non-Fiction, 1954-1974* (Madras: M. Seshchalam, 1976), p. 69.
14. French, p. 505.
15. Germaine Greer, *The Female Eunuch*, p. 320.
16. French, p. 506.
17. *Ibid*., p. 507.
18. Tara Ali Baig, *India's Woman Power*, pp. 130-31.
19. "Doris Lessing: The Free Woman's Commitment," Paul Schlueter, *Contemporary British Novelists*, ed. Charles Shapiro (1965; rpt. Carbondale; Southern Illinois University Press), p. 58.
20. Juliet Mitchell and Ann Oakley, ed. *The Rights and Wrongs of Women* (Harmondsworth: Penguin, 1976), p. 13.
21. G. Alison Raymond, *Half the World's People* (New York: Appleton-Century-Crofts, 1965), p. 70.
22. *Liberation Now*, ed. Deborah Babcox and Madeline Belkin (New York: Dell, 1971), p. 336.
23. Nayantara Sahgal, *Storm in Chandigarh*, p. 8.
24. Marcia P. Liu, "Continuity and Development in the Novels of Nayantara Sahgal," *Journal of Indian Writing in English*, 8, Nos. 1-2 (Jan.-July 1980), p. 51.
25. Nayantara Sahgal, *Rich Like Us*, p. 137.
26. Molly Hite, "(En)gendering Metafiction: Doris Lessing's Rehearsals for the Golden Notebook," *Modern Fiction Studies*, 34, No. 3 (Autumn 1988), p. 495.
27. A. R. Gupta, *Women in Hindu Society* (1976; rpt. New Delhi: Jyotsna, 1982), p. 68.
28. Nick Cole, " Divorce: A World of Epidemic," *The Tribune*, 23 August 1987, p. VII.
29. Dale Spender, *Women of Ideas and What Men Have Done to Them* (London: Routledge and Kegan Paul, 1982), p. 737.

I do not seek a victory over men. I do not wish to deny in full their values and their creations but I do want to deny, again and again, that their values and their creations are the only ones that society can outline. I want co-existence.

30. Fullerton, p. 460.
31. Cynthia Cockburn, quoted in Lynne Segal, *Is the Future Female? Troubled Thoughts on Contemporary Feminism*, pp. XIV-XV.

Conclusion

Both Nayantara Sahgal and Doris Lessing started writing before the feminist movement was launched in the sixties, yet they both independently take up issues concerning women which were to become major issues in the feminist movement. Despite their widely different cultural and social backgrounds both the novelists had certain similar experiences in their life as women. And we find that their female protagonists also, though they come from different classes and different social milieus, face similar problems in a sexist society. Unlike the stereotype women characters most of their protagonists were aware, assertive, intellecutally independent women who resent sexual discrimination against women which begins right from their childhood.

In the works of both Sahgal and Lessing there is a very sensitive depiction of the way women suffer due to the sexist bias in the patriarchal society which gives a subordinate position to women and always treats them as second-rate citizens. A woman's whole existence is seen in relation to the service she can render to a man. The subordination of woman begins even before her marriage when she is groomed by her parents, and ironically more often by mothers who are orthodox in their thinking, to grow into an attractive commodity that can have many uses for her husband in future. All the stress is laid on making her specificially feminine and an attempt is made to curb her independent spirits. While some girls bow to this conditioning, the more aware ones (like Nita) resent it and look for ways to answer the needs of their personalities; the bolder ones (like Martha) openly revolt against the kind of conditioning and take their own decisions over the issues of job and marriage. As such the novels uphold the feminist assertion that femininity is a cultural not biological construct.

A more pitiable and resentful phase of a woman's marginalization begins after her marriage. She is never recognized as an individual, an equal and a human being with her own needs and desires. She is usually seen as an object providing sexual pleasure to man, an asset as a decoration piece and a nursemaid to bring up the children and to shoulder all the responsibilities of the household. Her feelings and desires are completely ignored in marriage, while for man marriage means complete gratification on all fronts. He is also free to indulge in extra-marital relations without experiencing any sense of guilt while he can persecute his wife to any extent on mere suspicion of infidelity. Both Lessing and Sahgal expose the hypocrisy, meanness and double-standards of men in their novels. A married woman often feels greater loneliness than a single woman because her loneliness springs from the emotional injuries and sometimes physical injuries as well which she suffers at the hands of her husband. As a result woman, be it in the East or in the West, often feels suffocated and deprived in marriage. Even motherhood, which is seen as the final fulfilment of a woman and often craved for by woman, becomes a stifling factor in a woman's life. Children, instead of being the symbol of love between the parents, are often seen by husbands as instruments of gaining power over wives, because bringing up children makes women economically more vulnerable and emotionally more dependent on men.

Principles of self-interest and self-gratification rule the conduct of a man, be it in love or in marriage, while complete self-effacement and blind devotion to the husband are laid down as the principles that should govern the conduct of a woman. This unjust and uneven division of power and responsibilities is resented by both Sahgal and Lessing through their women characters.

Both the novelists portray the suffering and agony of women which results from uneven power-division in marriage, privileging one sex all the time and marginalizing the other. After having suffered in marriage which denies them any right to be an equal, independent individual, most of their women decide to break the bond of marriage. They decide to live on their own to fulfil the needs of their own self. Though divorce laws have made it easier now for women to take off the yoke of an unhappy marriage yet it does not put an end to woman's problems. After obtaining divorce she still has to struggle on various levels in the patriarchal set-up. A single woman is not accepted by society as a healthy, sane and normal person. She is seen as abnormal or deficient and is looked upon with suspicion. In the search for self-realization, she has to bear hardships on the economic level as well as the burden of bringing up the family does not allow her to pursue her job properly and often she does not have a very paying job, but she has heavier responsibilities because children are often left with mothers to be taken care of. However, Sahgal's and Lessing's women object not to wifehood or motherhood, but to the restraints traditionally accompanying these roles.

In the new phase of their life after divorce which does grant them freedom from constant oppression that they experienced in marriage, problems – emotional and material – again make the going tough for a single woman. They look for comfort, understanding and support in the company of other free women like them, but they also look for solace and emotional fulfilment in men with whom they develop friendship or whom they remarry.

Though basically the situations and experiences of Sahgal's and Lessing's women are the same, yet we also come across some difference in their responses, which could largely be due to the difference in their social milieus. While Lessing's women are bolder and rather Amazonian in asserting their individuality, Sahgal's women are rather slow in realizing their needs and then asserting their individuality. Sahgal's women, like their creator, hesitate for long before taking the final bold decisive step. One reason could be that Lessing's women are working, hence already exposed to the outer world and are also economically independent, while Sahgal's women, though well-educated, are largely housewives only. Even after divorce Sahgal's women feel rather diffident and depend more on others to help them out of their problems while Lessing's women can manage even on their own. While Lessing's single women enjoy more sexual freedom, Saghal's women take time even to get over the idea of divorce and do not feel so free to move about the world of men. In fact, even after divorce some of them again depend on men. On the other hand, Lessing's women depend more on women and find greater comfort and understanding among women, while with men their relationship often again brings suffering. Lessing's women are sexually very articulate and are very frank about their sexual needs. The common but private female experiences which were considered taboo have been frankly discussed by Lessing in her works. Sahgal's descriptions never become so defiant of conventions and she usually discusses the broader needs of independence and self-realization in her women.

Doris Lessing works out her feminist themes on a much broader canvas, juxtaposing the woman's question with larger political and existential issues. The quest for meaning, the search for self in Lessing's women is linked with larger issues than only sexist conflicts. As a result we find Lessing's women are politically more conscious, and socially very active. Sahgal, on the contrary, works out her feminist ideas in a limited world. The struggle for identity and fulfilment in her women is worked out more on a personal level within the family. There too we find she restricts herself to the study of women of one class, namely elite class. But then this is the class of which she has first-hand experience and she does make a close and sensitive study of the sufferings and responses of women of this class in a sexist society. Interestingly, the educated, affluent women in the more tradition-bound country India as depicted by Sahgal have similar uneasy, unfortunate experiences as the middle-class, working women living in the more permissive Western countries as depicted by Lessing; and women in both the worlds refuse to remain chained to their subordiante roles and defy the traditional norms in search of emancipation.

Though both Sahgal and Lessing reveal the suffering caused by the oppression of men, yet they are not against men as such; nor do they advocate a separatist stance. Even though many of their women opt out of marriage, yet they do long for the company of men and either have love affairs with them or get married again. Their women look for happiness and self-fulfilment again in a world shared by both the sexes. The call is for a recognition of woman as an equally important partner in marriage or in any other relationship. Her needs, her freedom, her personality, her individuality should be equally valued. The existing set-up with its uneven power-division will continue to bring suffering to women. And as long as one half of humanity suffers we cannot hope for a better world. Both the novelists envision a world which should be based on equality, sharing and harmony between the two sexes, where the needs, the functions, the virtues of women are valued equally along with those of men. Their vision thus is identical with that of the feminists in the eighties like Marilyn French, Dale Spender, Lynne Segal who also ask for a world built on equality of sexes, where male and female, masculine and feminine are valued equally, and act as complementary to each other, a world built on sharing and harmony.

Appendix

The Questionnaire

1. How would you like a comparative study of themes in your novels with Doris Lessing's? How many novels of Lessing have you read so far? Which one do you like best?
2. You have written two autobiographies about your childhood experiences and your married life before divorce. Would you like to recount experiences of your life after divorce and your second marriage in some other autobiography?
3. You always write of the aristocratic classes in your novels. What made you ignore characters from the lower classes?
4. From where did you conceive Raj's character and nice ideas about Christianity?
5. Why do you often portray male characters with discrimination? Why they are always shown as cruel characters like Som in *The Day in Shadow* and Inder in *Storm in Chandigarh?*
6. What was the idea behind creation of the character of Uma in *This Time of Morning*, who is different from other female characters of your novels?
7. Do you intend to experiment with any other literary style in your novels in near future?
8. Freedom struggle had tremendous impact on your upbringing. Often you recount those incidents in your interviews or articles of which you have already given good account in your autobiography, *Prison and Chocolate Cake*. Don't you feel like saying something about the situation of man in the modern chaotic world? How do you feel about it?
9. Would you like to be labelled as feminist?
10. Why most of your women characters after undergoing several traumatic experiences embrace marriage once again? Like Simrit in *The Day in Shadow*?
11. What is your vision of life?
12. After a long gap, your two novels have come out. Do you plan to write a new novel in near future? And about what?

The Response
April 5, 1987

1. I have read the following novels of Lessing: *A Proper Marriage, The Memoirs of a Survivor, The Good Terrorist, Briefing for a Descent into Hell* and part of *The Golden Notebook.* I like all these, but I think *Briefing* is masterly. I would be greatly interested in a comparative study of her work and mine.
2. I shall never write another autobiography. I should never have written the second one. I am less and less interested in myself, more and more in the fiction themes in my head that have to come out.
3. Do I? I think the question is wrongly put. One does not write about any class. One writes about the characters in one's hand. I think there is variety in my characters. The main ones come from an educated background because that happens to be my general experience.
4. My schooling was in Christian schools. I had to read the Bible. I learned a lot from it. In India the Christians as a community have made a big contribution – in education, in medicine and other areas – quietly, with dedication, and without fuss. They don't have the tortuous Hindu approach or the combative Muslim one. I think they have a straightforwardness we older denizens of the subcontinent lack. Raj had the traits of what I consider a good Christian!
5. What about Raj, and what about Vishal? Neither is "cruel." There are shades of good and bad in the women characters too, depending on what you consider good or bad. A reader thought Nita in *This Time of Morning* was a bad character because she had an affair with Kalyan. Kalyan himself is neither good nor bad, but a forceful one-track-minded sort.
6. A woman is not allowed to be a woman in orthodox thinking. She has to be "good" and good means virtuous in the sense of chaste. Uma was a woman with appetites that her husband couldn't satisfy, so she indulged themselves elsewhere. Men do it, and there's no comment. This happened to be a mismatched marriage (and there are many of those) in which the woman was the stronger, more independent character.
7. I have "experimented" in a sense in *Rich Like Us* and *Plans for Departure*. Both these are very different in sytle, and the former also in scope, from my previous novels.
8. This is a very big question. It is a chaotic world, which is why I write, to try and make some little order out of the chaos. It is why all writers write.

One cannot prescribe for the world, one can only arrange one's own life in a way that will be useful and worthwhile, and for artists, artistically fulfilling. Without being religious in the ritualistic or narrow sense, I do believe in the religious impulse. It is of great strength to me. In the end it is identification with the people and causes outside oneself that "redeems" one, makes one part of the world. I think my involvement with journalism and with civil liberties is a part of this effort.

9. Yes, I would, though I don't deserve the title. I have come to this awakening rather late, although I have personally always been independent-minded. That is not enough. I think if one cares, one must project, and ally oneself with one's beliefs. I think I do this more now as regards feminism.
10. Sonali does not in *Rich Like Us*. Simrit was a passive, un-feminist character. I think it was silly of her to re-marry,with all those children. But being the sort of character she was, it was natural for her to do so.
11. My "vision" for myself is that I should continue to write fiction, and that, personally, I should do no one any injury. In a broader sense, that the world should be the kind of place where people can pursue the peaceful arts, and be left in peace to pursue them, whether their work involves sewing a tablecloth or writing a book.
12. I have just completed a new novel titled *Mistaken Identity*. It, too, has a political background and takes place in the 1920's.

Bibliography

PRIMARY SOURCES

Lessing, Doris. *The Grass is Singing*. London: Michael Joseph, 1950; New York: T. Y. Crowell, 1950; London: Granada, 1980.

-----. *Martha Quest* (*Children of Violence*, Vol. I). London: Michael Joseph, 1952; New York: Simon and Schuster, 1964; London: Panther, 1984.

-----. *A Proper Marriage (Children of Violence,* Vol. II). London: Michael Joseph, 1954; New York: Simon and Schuster, 1964; London: Panther, 1977.

-----. *A Ripple from the Storm (Children of Violence*, Vol. III). London: Michael Joseph, 1958; New York: Simon and Schuster, 1966; London: Granada, 1981.

-----. *The Golden Notebook*. London: Michael Joseph, 1962; New York: Simon and Schuster, 1962; London: Granada, 1983.

Sahgal, Nayantara. *This Time of Morning.* New York: W. W. Norton, 1965; London: Victor Gollancz, 1965; Delhi: Hind Pocket Books, 1970.

-----. *Storm in Chandigarh*. New York: W.W. Norton, 1969; London: Chatto and Windus, 1969; Delhi: Hind Pocket Books, 1970.

-----. *The Day in Shadow*. New Delhi: Vikas, 1971; New York: W. W. Norton, 1972; London: London Magazine Editions, 1975; New Delhi: Bell, 1976.

-----. *A Situation in New Delhi*. London: London Magazine Editions, 1977; New Delhi: Himalaya, 1977.

-----. *Rich Like Us*. London: Heinemann, 1985.

SECONDARY SOURCES

(A) Other Writings by the authors

Lessing, Doris, *Going Home*. With drawings by Paul Hogarth. London: Michael Joseph, 1957. Rev. ed. London: Panther, 1968, and New York: Ballantine, 1968.

-----. *Each His Own Wilderness*. In *New English Dramatists: Three Plays*, ed. Elliot M. Browne. Harmondsworth, Middlesex: Penguin, 1959, pp. 11-95.
-----. *A Man and Two Women: Stories*. London: MacGibbon and Kee, 1963; New York: Simon and Schuster, 1963.
-----. *Landlocked (Children of Violence*, Vol. IV). London: MacGibbon and Kee, 1965; New York: Simon and Schuster, 1966.
-----. *The Four-Gated City* (*Children of Violence*, Vol. V). London: MacGibbon and Kee, 1969; New York: Alfred A. Knopf, 1969.
-----. *The Marriage Between Zones Three, Four and Five*. London: Jonathan Cape, 1980; London: Granada, 1981.
-----. *The Fifth Child*. London: Jonathan Cape, 1988.
Sahgal, Nayantara. *Prison and Chocolate Cake*. New York: Alfred A. Knopf, 1954; London: Victor Gollancz, 1954; Bombay: Jaico, 1964.
-----. *A Time to be Happy*. New York: Alfred A. Knopf, 1958; London: Victor Gollancz, 1958; Bombay: Jaico, 1963; New Delhi: Sterling, 1975.
-----. *From Fear Set Free*. New York: W.W. Norton, 1962; London: Victor Gollancz, 1962; Delhi: Hind Pocket Books, 1970.
-----. "Women – Persons or Possessions?" *The Hindustan Times*, 19 July 1970, p. IV.
-----. "Two Faces of a Novelist." *The Statesman*, 22 August 1970, p. 3.
-----. "Of Divorce and Hindu Woman." *The Hindustan Times*, 18 December 1971, p. 7.
-----. "The Woman in India: A Historical Perspective." *Span*, 15, No. 1 (Jan. 1974), pp. 35-37.
-----. "The Book I Enjoyed Writing Most." *Bhavan's Journal*, 20, No. 12 (6 Jan. 1974), pp. 41-44.
-----. "Adultery in Life and Literature." *The Sunday Standard*, 28 Sept. 1975, p. 8.
-----. *Plans for Departure*. London: Heinemann, 1986.
-----. *Mistaken Identity*. London: Heinemann, 1988.
-----. "Not 'a time to be happy' yet." *The Tribune*, 13 Feb. 1988, p. 16.
-----. "The Virtuous Woman." *The Tribune* (Saturday Plus), 24 December 1988, p. 1.

(B) Criticism on the authors

Books on Lessing

Brewster, Dorothy. *Doris Lessing.* New York: Twayne, 1965.

Rubenstein, Roberta. *The Novelistic Vision of Doris Lessing: Breaking the Forms of Consciousness*. Urbana: University of Illinois Press, 1979.

Sage, Lorna. *Doris Lessing.* London: Methuen, 1983.

Schlueter, Paul. T*he Novels of Doris Lessing.* Carbondale: Southern Illinois University Press, 1973.

Singleton, Mary Ann. *The City and the Veld*: *The Fiction of Doris Lessing.* Lewisburg, Pa: Bucknell University Press, 1977.

Thorpe, Michael. *Doris Lessing's Africa.* New York: Holmes and Meier, 1978.

Articles on Lessing

Allen, Orphia Jane. "Structure and Motif in Doris Lessing's *A Man and Two Women.*" *Modern Fiction Studies,* 26 (Spring 1980), pp. 63-74.

Barnouw, Dagmar. "Disorderly Company: From *The Golden Notebook* to *The Four-Gated City.*" *Contemporary Literature,* 14 (Autumn 1973), pp. 491-514.

Bazin, Nancy Topping. "The Moment of Revelation in *Martha Quest* and the Comparable Moments by Two Modernists." *Modern Fiction Studies*, 26 (Spring 1980), pp. 87-98.

Bergonzi, Bernard. "In Pursuit of Doris Lessing." *New York Review of Books*, 11 February 1965, pp. 12-14.

Bolling, Douglas, "Structure and Themes in *Briefing for a Descent into Hell.*" *Contemporary Literature* (Autumn 1973), pp. 550-64.

Brooks, Ellen W. "Fragmentation and Integration: A Study of Doris Lessing's Fiction." *Dissertation Abstracts International*, 32 (1971), 3989-90A.

Burkom, Selma R. "A Doris Lessing Checklist." *Critique*, II, No. 1 (1969), pp. 69-81.

-----. "'Only Connect': Form and Content in the Works of Doris Lessing." *Critique*, II, No. 1 (1969), pp. 51-68.

Campbell, Elaine. "The Life Passages of Kate Brown: Doris Lessing's Neglected Novel." *World Literature Written in English*, 21, No. 2 (Autumn 1982), pp. 411-15.

Carey, Alfred Augustine. "Doris Lessing: The Search for Reality. A Study of the Major Themes in Her Novels." *Dissertation Abstracts International*, 26 (1965), 3297A.

Carey, John L. "Art and Reality in *The Golden Notebook*." *Contemporary Literature*, 14 (Autumn 1973), pp. 437-56.

Cederstrom, Loreler. "Doris Lessing's Use of Satire in *The Summer Before the Dark*." *Modern Fiction Studies*, 26, No.1 (Spring 1980), pp. 131-45.

Draine, Betsy. "Changing Frames: Doris Lessing's *Memoirs of a Survivor*." *Studies in the Novel*, II, No. 1 (Spring 1979), pp. 51-62.

Driver, C.J. "Profile 8: Doris Lessing." *New Review*, I (November 1974), pp. 17-23.

Duyfhuizen, Bernard. "On the Writing of Future-History: Beginning the Ending in Doris Lessing's *The Memoirs of a Survivor*." *Modern Fiction Studies*, 26 (Spring 1980), pp. 147-56.

Fishburn, Katherine, "The Dialectics of Perception in Doris Lessing's *Retreat to Innocence*." *World Literature Written in English*, 21, No. 2 (Autumn 1982), pp. 416-33.

Fuoroli, Caryn. "Doris Lessing's 'Game': Referential Langauge and Fictional Form." *Twentieth Century Literature*, 27, No. 2 (Summer 1981), pp. 146-67.

Gottlieb, Lois C. and Wendy Kutner. "Colonialism as Metaphor and Experience in *The Grass is Singing* and *Surfacing*." *Awakened Conscience: Studies in Commonwealth Literature*, ed. C.D. Narasimhaiah. New Delhi: Sterling, 1978, pp. 307-14.

Hardin, Nancy S. "Doris Lessing and the Sufi Way." *Contemporary Literature*, 14 (Autumn 1973), pp. 565-81

-----. "Sufi Teaching Story and Doris Lessing." *Twentieth Century Literature*, 23 (October 1977), pp. 314-26.

Hite, Molly. "(En)gendering Metafiction: Doris Lessing's Rehearsals for *The Golden Notebook*." *Modern Fiction Studies*, 34, No. 3 (Autumn 1988), pp. 481-99.

Howe, Florence. "A Conversation with Doris Lessing (1966)." *Contemporary Literature*, 14 (Autumn 1973), pp. 418-36.

Kaplan, Sydney Janet. "The Limits of Consciousness in the Novels of Doris Lessing." *Contemporary Literature*, 14 (Autumn 1973), pp. 536-49.

-----. "Passionate Portrayal of Things to Come: Doris Lessing's Recent Fiction." *Twentieth Century Women Novelists*, ed. Thomas F. Staley. London: Macmillan, 1982, pp. 1-15.

Karl, Frederick R. "Doris Lessing in the Sixties: The New Anatomy of Melancholy." *Contemporary Literature*, 13 (Winter 1972), pp. 15-33.

Krouse, Agate Nesaule, "A Doris Lessing Checklist." *Contemporary Literature,* 14 (Autumn 1973), pp. 590-97.

Magic, Michael L. "Doris Lessing and Romanticism." *College English*, 38 (February 1977), pp. 531-52.

Manion, Eileen. "'Not About the Colour Problem': Doris Lessing's Portrayal of the Colonial Order." *World Literature in English*, 21, No. 2 (Autumn 1982), pp. 432-55.

Marchino, Lois, "The Search for Self in the Novels of Doris Lessing." *Studies in the Novel*, 4 (Summer 1972), pp. 252-61.

Morgan, Ellen. "Alienation of the Woman Writer in *The Golden Notebook.*" *Contemporary Literature*, 14 (Autumn 1973), pp. 471-80.

Parrinder, Patrick. "Descents into Hell: The Later Novels of Doris Lessing." *Critical Quarterly*, 22, No. 4 (Winter 1980), pp. 5-25.

Pickering, Jean. "Marxism and Madness: The Two Faces of Doris Lessing's Myth." *Modern Fiction Studies*, 26 (Spring 1980), pp. 17-30.

Pratt, Annis. "Introduction." *Contemporary Literature*, 14 (Autumn 1973), pp. 413-17.

Sarvan, Charles and Liebetrant Sarvan. "D.H. Lawrence and Doris Lessing's *The Grass is Singing.*" *Modern Fiction Studies*, 24 (Winter 1978-79), pp. 533-37.

Scanlan, Margaret. "Memory and Continuity in the Series Novel: The Example of *Children of Violence.*" *Modern Fiction Studies*, 26 (Spring 1980), pp. 75-85.

Schlueter, Paul. "Doris Lessing: The Free Woman's Commitment." *Contemporary British Novelists,* ed. Charles Shapiro. Carbondale: Southern Illinois Univ. Press, 1965, pp. 48-61.

-----, ed. *A Small Personal Voice: Essays, Reviews, Interviews*. New York: Random, 1975.

Seligman, Dee. "The Four-Faced Novelist." *Modern Fiction Studies,* 26 (Spring 1980), pp. 3-16.

Spilka, Mark. "Lessing and Lawrence: The Battle of the Sexes." *Contemporary Literature*, 16, No. 2 (Spring 1975), pp. 218-40.

Sprague, Claire. "'Without Contraries is no Progression': Lessing's *The Four-Gated City*." *Modern Fiction Studies*, 26 (Spring 1980), pp. 99-116.

Stern, C. Frederick. "The Changing 'Voice' of Lessing's Characters: From Politics to Science Fiction." *World Literature Written in English*, 21, No. 2 (Autumn 1982), pp. 456-66.

Sukenick, Lynn. "Feeling and Reason in Doris Lessing's Fiction." *Contemporary Literature*, 14 (Autumn 1973), pp. 515-35.

Sullivan, Alvin. "*The Memoirs of a Survivor*: Lessing's Notes Towards a Supreme Fiction." *Modern Fiction Studies*, 26 (Spring 1980), pp. 157-62.

Taubman, Robert. "Doris Lessing and Nadine Gordimer." *The New Pelican Guide to English Literature*, Vol. 8: The Present, ed. Boris Ford. Harmondsworth: Penguin, 1983, pp. 233-44.

Zax, Michele W. "*The Grass is Singing*: A Little Novel about the Emotions." *Contemporary Literature*, 14 (Autumn 1973), pp. 481-90.

Books on Sahgal

Jain, Jasbir. *Nayantara Sahgal*. New Delhi: Arnold-Heinemann, 1978.

Kohli, Suresh. *Nayantara Sahgal and the Craft of Fiction*. New Delhi: Vikas, 1972.

Krishna Rao, A.V. *Nayantara Sahgal: A Study of Her Fiction and Non-Fiction*. Madras : N. Seshachalam, 1976.

Mukherjee, Meenakshi. *The Twice Born Fiction: Themes and Techniques of the Indian Novel in English*, 2nd ed., 1971; rpt. New Delhi: Arnold-Heinemann, 1974. (Chapter 3 "The Making of a Nation" contains a discussion of Sahgal's *A Time to be Happy*.)

Naik, M.K. *A History of Indian English Literature*. New Delhi: Sahitya Akademi, 1982.

Parameswaran, Uma. *A Study of Representative Indo-English Novelists*. New Delhi: Vikas, 1976.

Shirwadkar, Meena. *Image of Woman in Indo-Anglian Fiction*. New Delhi: Sterling, 1979.

Srinivasa Iyengar, K.S. *Indian Writing in English*. New Delhi: Asia, 1962; 1983.

Articles on Sahgal

Asnani, Shyam M. "East-West Encounter in Nayantara Sahgal's Novels." *Commonwealth Quarterly,* 3 (Dec. 1978), pp. 188-98.

-----. "New Morality in the Modern Indo-English Novel." *Explorations in Modern Indo-English Fiction*, ed. R.K. Dhawan. New Delhi: Bahri, 1982,pp. 59-70.

-----. "Portrayal of Man-Woman Relationship in the Novels of Nayantara Sahgal." *Kakatiya Journal of English Studies*, 3, No. 1 (1978), pp. 151-65.

-----. "*Prison and Chocolate Cake*—A Study." *The Journal of Indian Writing in English*, 7, No. 1 (Jan. 1979), pp. 47-60.

-----. "Form and Technique in Nayantara Sahgal's Novels." *Literary Endeavour*, 1, No.3 (Jan. 80), pp. 41-50.

-----. "The Novels of Nayantara Sahgal." *Indian Literature*, 16, Nos. 1-2 (Jan. & June 1973), pp. 36-39.

Baweja, Harinder and Vijay Dutt. "Nayantara Sahgal's Brush with History." *Probe*, May 1986, pp. 14-17.

Chinneswararao, C. J. "Nayantara Sahgal's *A Situation in New Delhi:* A Study." *Commonwealth Quarterly*, 3 (Dec. 1978), pp. 154-61.

Jain, Jasbir. "The Politics of Hinduism in the Novels of Nayantara Sahgal." *Littcrit*, 2, No. 2 (December 1976), pp. 45-47.

-----. "The Aesthetics of Morality: Sexual Relations in the Novels of Nayantara Sahgal." *Journal of Indian Writing in English*, 6, No. 1 (Jan. 1978), pp. 41-48.

-----. "The Political Novel and the Contemporary Scene in Indo-English Fiction." *Indian Book Chronicle*, 13, No. 3 (March 1988), pp. 62- 65.

-----. "Politics and Personality." *Indian Express*, 26 Feburary 1989, p. 5.

John, Usha. "Nayantara Sahgal" (Profile). *Femina*, 4 Feb. 1972, p. 13.

-----. "Political Fiction." *Indian and Foreign Review*, 15 June 1979, pp. 24-25.

Jussawalla, Feroza. "Of Cabbages and Kings: *This Time of Morning* and *Storm in Chandigarh* by Nayantara Sahgal." *Journal of Indian Writing in English*, 5, No. 1 (Jan. 1977), pp. 43-50 .

Liu, Marcia P. "Continuity and Development in the Novels of Nayantara Sahgal." *Journal of Indian Writing in English*, 8, Nos. 1-2 (Jan.-July 1980), pp. 45-52

Mukherjee, Meenakshi. "Curate's Egg." *Quest*, 77 (July- August 1972), pp. 92-94.

Naik, M.K. "Post Independence Indo-English Fiction." *Littcrit*, 8, No. 1 (June 1982), pp. 7-12.

Narayan, Shyamala A. "Nayantara Sahgal: An Assessment." *Commonwealth Fiction*, ed. R.K. Dhawan. New Delhi: Classical, 1988, Vol. I, pp. 268-70.

Ram, Atma "Interview with Nayantara Sahgal." *Interviews with Indian English Writers*. Calcutta: Writers Workshop, 1983, pp. 45-48.

----. "Oppressed Like Us." *The Tribune*, 14 Nov. 1987, p. 4.

Sarma, Krishna S. "Positive Living; A brief examination of some features of Nayantara Sahgal's *Storm in Chandigarh* and *A Day in Shadow*." *Kakatiya Journal of English Studies*, 3, No.1 (1978), pp. 166-78.

Sarma, M.N. "Nayantara Sahgal's Novels: Some Thematic Concerns." *Journal of Indian Writing in English*, 4, No.1 (Jan. 1976), pp. 35-44.

Sharma, D.R. "Nayantara Sahgal." *The Sunday Tribune*, 26 March 1978, p. 6.

Sinha, Lakshmi. "Nayantara Sahgal's *Storm in Chandigarh:* A Search for Values." *Studies in Indian Fiction in English*, ed. G.S. Balarama Gupta. Gulbarga: JIWE Publications, 1987, pp. 104-12.

(C) Feminism

Books

Altekar, A.S. *The Position of Women in the Hindu Civilization: From Pre-History to the Present Day*. New Delhi: Motilal Banarsidas, 1962.

Asthana, Pratima. *Women's Movement in India.* Delhi: Vikas, 1974.

Augustine, S., ed. *Indian Family in Transition*. New Delhi: Vikas, 1982.

Baig, Tara Ali. *India's Woman Power*. New Delhi: S. Chand, 1976.

Chafe, William H. *Women and Equality*. New York: Oxford University Press, 1977.

Chattopadhyaya, Kamaladevi. *Indian Women's Battle for Freedom*. New Delhi: Abhinav, 1983.

Cixous, Helene and Catherine Clement. *La Jeune Nee*. Paris: Union Generale d' Editions, 1975. Translated as *The Newly Born Woman* by Betsy Wing. Minneapolis: Univ. of Minnesota, 1986.

De Beauvoir, Simone. *The Second Sex*. Trans. and ed. H. M. Parshley, 1953; rpt. Harmondsworth: Penguin, 1983.

Desai, Neera. *Women in Modern India*. Bombay: Vora, 1977.

----- and Vibhuti Patel. *Indian Women: Change and Challenge in the International Decade* 1975-1985. Bombay: Popular, 1985.

----- and Maithreyi Krishnaraj. *Women and Society in India*. Delhi: Ajanta, 1987.

Dworkin, Andrea. *Intercourse*. London: Martin Secker and Warburg, 1987.

Eisenstein, Hester. *Contemporary Feminist Thought*. Boston: Hall, 1983.

Ellman, Mary. *Thinking about Women*. New York: Harcourt, Brace Jovanovich, 1968.

Engels, F. *The Origin of the Family, Private Property and the State*. 1884; rpt. Moscow: Progress, 1972.

Everett, Jana Matson. *Women and Social Change in India*. New Delhi: Heritage, 1981.

Figes, Eva. *Patriarchal Attitudes*. London: Faber and Faber, 1970.

Firestone, Shulamith. *The Dialectic of Sex*. New York: William Morrow, 1970.

French, Marilyn. *Shakespeare's Division of Experience*. 1982; rpt. London: Abacus, 1983.

-----. *Beyond Power: On Women, Men and Morals*. London: Abacus, 1986.

Friedan, Betty. *The Feminine Mystique*, 1963; rpt. Harmondsworth: Penguin, 1965.

-----. *The Second Stage*. New York: Summit, 1981.

Fullerton, Gail Putney. *Survival in Marriage*. Illinois: Dryden Press Hinsdale, 1977.

Gilbert, Sandra M. *The War of the Words*. New Haven: Yale Univ. Press, 1988. Vol. 1 of *No Man's Land: The Place of the Woman Writer in the Twentieth Century* (1 vol. to date).

----- and Susan Gubar. *The Madwoman in the Attic: The Woman Writer and the Nineteenth-Century Literary Imagination*. New Haven: Yale Univ. Press, 1979.

Gornick, Vivian and Barbara K. Moran, eds. *Woman in Sexist Society: Studies in Power and Powerlessness*. New York: New American Library, Mentor Books, 1972.

Greer, Germaine. *The Female Eunuch*. 1970; rpt. St. Albana: Paladin, 1976.

-----. *Sex and Destiny*. London: Secker and Warburg, 1984.

-----. *The Madwoman's Underclothes: Essays and Occasional Writings 1968-85*. London: Picador, 1986.

Gupta, A. R. *Women in Hindu Society*. 1976; rpt. New Delhi: Jyotsna, 1982.

Haralambos, Michael and Robin Heald. *Sociology: Themes and Perspectives*. 1980; rpt. Delhi: Oxford University Press, 1983.

Jain, Devaki. *Women's Quest for Power: Five Case Studies*. New Delhi: Vikas, 1980.

-----, ed. *Indian Women*. New Delhi: Publications Division, Ministry of I & B, 1975.

----- and Nirmala Bannerjee. *Tyranny of the Household: Women in Poverty*. Delhi: Shakti Books, Vikas, 1985.

Janeway, Elizabeth. *Man's World, Woman's Place*. New York: William Morrow, 1971.

Jayal, Shakambari. *The Status of Women in the Epics*. Delhi: Motilal Banarsidass, 1966.

Jayawardhane, Kumari. *Feminism and Nationalism in the Third World in the 19th and early 20th Centuries*. Hague: Inst. of Social Studies, 1982.

Jha, Akhileshwar. *Modernization and the Hindu Socio-Culture*. Delhi: B. R. Publishing Corporation, 1978.

Kapadia, K.M. *Marriage and Family in India*. Bombay: Oxford Univ. Press, 1966.

Kapur, Promilla. *Marriage and the Working Woman in India*. Delhi: Vikas, 1970.

-----. *Love, Marriage, Sex and the Indian Woman*. 1976; rpt. New Delhi: Orient Paperbacks, 1980.

Kaushik, Susheela, ed. *Women's Oppression: Patterns and Perspectives*. New Delhi: Shakti Books, Vikas, 1985.

Kopp, Claire B., ed. *Becoming Female: Perspectives on Development*. New York: Plenum Press, 1979.

Kuppuswamy, B. *Social Change in India*. 1972; rpt. New Delhi: Vikas, 1982.

Lantz, Herman R. and Eloise C. Snyder. *Marriage: An Examination of the Man-Woman Relationship*. New York: John Wiley, 1962.

Madhavananda, Swami and Ramesh Chandra Majumdar, eds. *Great Women of India*. Almora: Advaita Ashrama, 1953.

Majumdar, Vina, ed. *Symbols of Power: Women in Changing Society*. Bombay: Allied, 1979.

Manault, Gail, ed. *The Extended Family: Women and Political Participation in India and Pakistan*. New Delhi: Chanakya, 1981.

Marder, Herbert. *Feminism and Art: A Study of Virginia Woolf*. Chicago: The Univ. of Chicago Press, 1968.

Mehta, Rama. *Divorced Hindu Woman*. Delhi: Vikas,1975.

Millett, Kate. *Sexual Politics*. 1969; rpt: London: Rupert Hart-Davis, 1971.

Mitchell, Juliet. *Women's Estate*. New York: Vintage, 1973.

-----. *Psychoanalysis and Feminism*. Harmondsworth: Pelican, 1975.

----- and Ann Oakley, eds. *The Rights and Wrongs of Women*. Harmondsworth: Penguin, 1976.

Mukherjee, Ila. *Social Status of North Indian Women*. Agra: Shivalal Agarwal, 1972.

Nayak, Jessie B. Tellis. *Indian Womanhood Then and Now*. Indore: Satprakashan Sanchar Kendra, 1983.

Phadnis, Urmila and Indira Malani, eds. *Women of the World*. New Delhi: Vikas, 1978.

Raymond, G. Alison. *Half the World's People*. New York: Appleton-Century, 1965.

Rowbotham, Sheila. *Women, Resistance and Revolution*. New York: Pantheon, 1972.

Segal, Lynne. *Is the Future Female?: Troubled Thoughts on Contemporary Feminism*. London: Virago, 1987.

Sircar, Manjushri Chakki. *Feminism in a Traditional Society*. Ghaziabad: Shakti Books, Vikas, 1984.

D'Souza, Alfred, ed. *Women in Contemporary India*. 2nd ed., 1977; rpt. New Delhi: Manohar, 1980.

Swamy, Shanta Krishna. *Glimpses of Women in India*. New Delhi: Ashish, 1983.

Wagner, Geoffrey. *Five for Freedom: A Study of Feminism in Fiction*. London: George Allen and Unwin, 1972.

Watt, George. *The Fallen Women in the Nineteenth Century English Novel*. London: Croomhelm, 1984.

Wollstonecraft, Mary. *A Vindication of the Rights of Woman*. 1792; ed. Miriam Kramnick, rpt. Harmondsworth: Penguin, 1975.

-----. *Mary and the Wrongs of Woman*. 1788, 1798; rpt. Oxford: Oxford Univ. Press, 1983.

Articles

Baig, Tara Ali. "Who Says the Sati System is Dead." *Femina*, 23 Dec. 1983--7 Jan. 1984, p. 58.

Bhatia, B.S. "Children of Broken Marriages." *The Tribune*, 24 July 1988, p. III.

Carden, Maren Lockwood. "Why do American Women Want Liberation." *Span*, 16, No. 10 (Oct. 1975), pp. 6-8.

Chenoy, Polly N. "Why are You Crying We are Sisters: Feminism American and Indian." *Indian Journal of American Studies*, 13, No. 2 (July 1983), pp. 165-78.

Cole, Nick. "Divorce: A World Epidemic." *The Tribune*, 23 August 1987, p. VII.

Gordon, Elizabeth. "Women of Asia." *Contemporary Review*, 229, No. 1330 (Nov. 1976), pp. 266-68.

Hall, Suzanne. "Feminist Writing." *Literature Alive*, 1, No. 2 (Sept. 1987), pp. 1-14.

Kang, Diljit Kaur. "Sati: Barbarous Survival." *The Tribune*, 4 October 1987, p. III.

Kanwar, Asha S. "A Literature of Their Own: An Experiment in Feminist Pedagogy." *Focus on English*, 4, No. 4 (October 1988), pp. 8-15.

Kapp, Isa. "Women's Liberation in America: Some Acknowledgements and Some Reservations." *Span*, 15, No. 1 (Jan. 1974), pp. 21-27.

Lewis, Jane. "The Debate on Sex and Class." *New Left Review*, No. 149 (Jan./Feb. 1985), pp. 108-21.

Maroney, Jon Heather. "Feminism at Work." *New Left Review*, No. 141 (Sept./Oct. 1983), pp. 50-71.

Moi, Toril. "Feminist Literary Criticism." *Modern Literary Theory: A Comparative Introduction*, ed. Ann Jefferson and David Robey, 1982; rpt. London: B.T. Batsford, 1986, pp. 204-21.

Novarra, V.A. "International Women's Year 1975." *Contemporary Review*, 226, No. 1313 (June 1975), pp. 316-20.

Patel, Vibhuti. "Women's Liberation in India." *New Left Review*, No. 153 (Sept./Oct. 1985), pp. 75-87.

Saran, Sathya. "Licence to Kill." *Femina*, 8-22 Sept. 1987, pp. 27-28.

Vasudev, Uma. "Women." *Change and Conflict in India*, ed. Romesh Thapar. Madras: The Macmillan, 1978, pp. 61-70.

Weir, Angela and Elizabeth Wilson. "The British Women's Movement." *New Left Review*, No. 148 (Nov./Dec. 1984), pp. 74-103.

Wollheim, Richard. "Psychoanalysis and Feminism." *New Left Review*, No. 93 (Sept./Oct. 1975), pp. 61-69.

(D) Miscellaneous Works

Abercrombie, Nicholas, Stephen Hill and Bryan S. Turner. *Dictionary of Sociology*. Harmondsworth: Penguin, 1984.

Anand, Mulk Raj. *Selected Short Stories*. Ed. M. K. Naik. New Delhi: Arnold Heinemann, 1977.

Erikson, Erik H. *Identity: Youth and Crisis*. London: Faber and Faber, 1968.

Hawthorne, Nathaniel. *The Scarlet Letter and Selected Tales*. 1850; rpt. Harmondsworth: Penguin, 1982.

Ibsen, Henrik. *The League of Youth, A Doll's House, The Lady from the Sea*. Trans. Peter Watts, 1965; rpt. Harmondsworth: Penguin, 1980.

James, Henry. *The Portrait of a Lady*. 1881; rpt. Harmondsworth: Penguin, 1982.

Mukherjee, Meenakshi. *Realism and Reality: The Novel and Society in India*. Delhi: Oxford University Press, 1985.

Ramamurti, K.S. *Rise of the Indian Novel in English*. New Delhi: Sterling, 1987.

O'Sullivan, Tim, et. al. *Key Concepts in Communication*. London: Methuen, 1983.

Toffler, Alvin. *Previews and Premises*. 1983; rpt. London: Pan, 1984.

Trilling, Lionel. *Sincerity and Authenticity*. 1971; rpt. Cambridge: Harvard Univ. Press, 1973.

Wilkins, W. J. *Hindu Mythology: Vedic and Puranic*. 1882; rpt. New Delhi: Rupa, 1979.

Index